Service-Learning...
by Degrees

Service-Learning...
by Degrees

How Adolescents

Can Make a Difference

in the Real World

Alice Terry | Jann Bohnenberger

HEINEMANN
Portsmouth, NH

Heinemann
A division of Reed Elsevier, Inc.
361 Hanover Street
Portsmouth, NH 03801–3912
www.heinemann.com

Offices and agents throughout the world

The authors and publisher wish to thank those who have generously given permission
to reprint borrowed material:

"Kids Who Saved a Dying Town" by Bruce B. Henderson. From *Reader's Digest*, September 1987. Reprinted with permission of the publisher.

Library of Congress Cataloging-in-Publication Data
Terry, Alice W.
Service-learning . . . by degrees : how adolescents can make a difference in the real
world / Alice W. Terry, Jann E. Bohnenberger.
p. cm.
Includes bibliographical references.
ISBN-13: 978-0-325-00986-5
ISBN-10: 0-325-00986-4
1. Student service. 2. Teenage volunteers in social service. I. Bohnenberger,
Jann E. II. Title.

LC220.5.T37 2007
361.3'7—dc22   2006027159

Editor: Danny Miller
Production: Elizabeth Valway
Cover design: Night & Day Design
Composition: Kim Arney
Manufacturing: Jamie Carter

Printed in the United States of America on acid-free paper
11 10 09 08 07 VP 1 2 3 4 5

Dedicated to Dr. E. Paul and J. Pansy
Torrance whose creativity, vision, and
belief in children inspired this book. It is
our hope to enable youth to make a
difference in their community through
positive social action, a vision inspired and
encouraged by Pansy and Paul.

Contents

Appendix A Reproducible Handouts and Transparency Masters 125

Creative Problem Solving:

- *Idea Jot Board . . . Brainstorming Ideas*
- *Abstract Shape*
- *The Community-Action Model*
- *Challenges Jot Board*
- *Action Ideas Jot Board*
- *Action Ideas Evaluation Matrix*

Choice and Voice:

- *Facilitator's Group*
- *Correspondence Action Group*
- *Public Relations Action Group*
- *Media Action Group*
- *Documentation Action Group*
- *Digital Coordinator*
- *Press Secretary*
- *File Clerk*
- *Journalist*
- *Scrapbook Coordinator*
- *Job Selection Form for Action Groups*
- *T-shirt Design*

Communication Skills:

- *Designing Action Stationery*
- *Telephone Tips*
- *Let's Talk*
- *Meeting Tips*
- *Press Conference*
- *Role-playing the Action*
- *Our Skit Action Plan*

Acknowledgments

To all those who have influenced us and supported our endeavors to enable all students to take positive action in their communities through service-learning, we owe a giant debt of gratitude. We would like to acknowledge and thank the students whose words adorn the pages of this book with the commitment and passion they felt as they took positive action in their communities. We especially acknowledge and appreciate our wonderful families—our husbands, parents, and children, who have understood our dream, believed in us, and kept the home fires burning very brightly.

Chapter One

Introduction to Service-Learning

The following story originally appeared in *Reader's Digest* in 1987. It chronicles the first service-learning project one of the authors was involved in—actually the project predated the term *service-learning*. This is a wonderful story to share with students as you embark on your first service-learning experience. This amazing story of courage and determination is very inspiring and shows what real kids can do in the real world through service-learning. Chapters 2, 3, and 4 begin with a vignette from this story in order to explain the three levels of service-learning identified in this book.

"The Kids Who Saved a Dying Town"

On a Wednesday afternoon in September 1984, five gifted sixth-graders and their teacher walked through downtown Royston, Georgia. "Look at those ugly old buildings!" Julinna Oxley exclaimed, pointing to two adjoining boarded-up structures that appeared as if they might topple in a strong wind.

"Why doesn't someone do something about them?" asked Matt Wilson.

Julinna was writing down what the students saw on their "awareness walk." She noted the addresses of the offending buildings, located only a few doors from the intersection of Royston's main streets. During the next hour, Julinna's list grew, and the kids became angered by what they observed. Six of the 36 buildings in the prime downtown area were vacant. There was litter everywhere. Overgrown weeds. Peeling paint.

Then the students came to another eyesore: a pile of junked cars and trucks next to a city park. "Why does the city allow it?" Judi Gurley wondered.

Alice Terry, their young, energetic teacher, had an idea: why not assign the class to find the answers?

Royston, population 2,650, is located 100 miles northeast of Atlanta and was founded in 1875. Once a thriving cotton center, it became a town that time had passed by. Royston's one claim to fame: baseball immortal Ty Cobb called it home. Now many natives had to move elsewhere for work. Residents drove to neighboring towns to shop.

To Alice Terry's students, it was obvious that downtown Royston was dying. And no one was doing anything to stop the slide. When they returned to their classroom at Royston Elementary School, the students were unusually quiet. One of them said later, "I felt so sorry for Royston, I wanted to cry."

Alice Terry, married to the school's principal, had taught this group of gifted students for several years. Twice a week, on Wednesday and Friday afternoons, her job was to find special ways to inspire these youngsters, who needed stimulation beyond their regular schoolwork. She called this her *Challenge Class*.

Now, sliding a chair over to the low table where the kids were sitting, she asked a question. "Okay, we identified some of our town's problems. What can we do to save Royston?" Action, not talk, was what she graded the students on. "Someone has to tow the junked cars away," said Judi Gurley.

"Maybe we can get the owner of those two boarded-up buildings to fix them," added another student.

Alice scribbled furiously to keep up with the ideas that sprang forth. These kids were bright and talented. Brandee Braswell was a born conciliator, adept at dealing with the public. Derrick Gable excelled in organization. Judi Gurley often played devil's advocate, taking an opposing view for the sake of discussion. Julinna Oxley was the natural leader with a talent for transforming ideas into sensible action. Matt Wilson was the artist of the group.

Calling themselves RIPPLES—because they wanted to start a ripple effect among townspeople to revitalize Royston—the students decided to write public officials who could help. When the RIPPLES Gang learned that the owner of the two dilapidated buildings had refused either to sell or to renovate, they sent him a sharply worded letter: "The buildings are a fire hazard. Before we contact the state fire marshal, we strongly urge you to fix them up or sell them to someone who will."

One of the students suggested they also write to the owner of the auto-wrecking business about the rusting cars and trucks.

When the class learned the junked vehicles were on land belonging to the railroad, they decided to alert railroad officials. Alice

Terry wrote, "I am a teacher of gifted students who are doing a year-long project on the revitalization of our downtown. Your property, leased by King's Auto to park wrecked cars and trucks, is an eyesore. We ask that you take immediate action."

Things were beginning to stir in Royston. But a few merchants were upset because the students were bringing civic problems to the public's attention. This seemed "too negative" to them.

In January the students received a late Christmas present. Alice told them, "I have good news. Those two old buildings went up for sale yesterday!"

The kids were stunned momentarily. Then they started shouting, "We did it! They listened to us!"

"Congratulations!" Alice called out over the clamor. "All right," she said. "What should we do next?"

"Let's ask the town to buy the buildings and restore them," one pupil suggested.

The following week the RIPPLES Gang trooped off to ask the city council to pay for a survey of residents and merchants. After two weeks of study, Mayor John Beard called Alice. "Tell your students we'll do it."

One questionnaire asked residents, "How often do you shop in downtown Royston?" "What kinds of businesses do you patronize?" "If new retail establishments were developed, what types of stores and services would you use?"

The merchants were asked, "How would you rate the downtown area for quality of eating places, parking, cleanliness of streets?" "What do you think is the primary reason why people don't shop in Royston?" "What kinds of improvements would you like to see?"

The results showed that the residents were discouraged from shopping in Royston because of limited merchandise, poor store appearance, and a lack of competitive prices. Nearly all residents said they would shop in Royston if the downtown area was improved. The RIPPLES Gang was now sure that the townspeople were with them.

In early February, Alice found a letter from the railroad in her mailbox. That afternoon, she opened it in front of the class. Inside was a copy of the railroad's certified letter to King's Auto, demanding that the junked cars be moved from railroad property immediately. The students cheered when Alice finished. Within a few weeks, there wasn't a junked vehicle in sight.

Meanwhile the group found a turn-of-the-century picture of the two dilapidated buildings, then well maintained and sturdy. Matt, the artist, went to work on a drawing to show how the structures might look restored.

Next the kids fashioned a proposal for the city to buy the buildings, and then they went to the city council. "You can buy both buildings for a few thousand dollars," Alice told council members.

"There would be an additional expense in restoring them. But the Chamber of Commerce needs an office, and you can rent the other one to bring in revenue."

Two weeks later, Brandee, whose father was on the city council, came to class with news that the council had voted to buy the two buildings. The students jumped out of their chairs, exchanging hugs.

"It's like we're adults instead of kids," one student said. "People are listening to our ideas."

But then came bad news. "The buildings were sold to someone else," John Beard reported to Alice Terry one day. "We didn't move quickly enough. A person named Gerald Carey bought them."

"That's not fair!" Matt shouted when he heard the news.

"It's not the end of the world," Alice said quietly. "What did you set out to accomplish?"

"To restore the buildings," Julinna answered.

"Right," Alice said. "Maybe you can still accomplish that." "Let's go talk to the new owner. Maybe we can get *him* to restore the buildings," Brandee suggested.

During a phone conversation with Alice Terry, Gerald Carey made his position clear. "No bunch of kids is going to tell me what to do with my property," he warned. But he grudgingly agreed to talk with them.

At the meeting, the kids began telling him what they had in mind. Carey, a native of Royston, was impressed by Matt's sketches. Half an hour later, he was smiling and agreeing how nice the buildings would look restored. "Can I keep these drawings to show my contractor so he'll know what I want done?" he finally asked.

The "Detour—Road Closed" signs went up on Royston's main streets the afternoon of May 15, 1985. Traffic was diverted as a horde of children descended on the downtown area. Their mission: to clean up the city's cluttered streets.

When the idea of a work detail was first discussed, one of Alice's fellow teachers scoffed, "No kid is going to volunteer for cleanup work." But the RIPPLES talked up the project and presented a skit to fourth-, fifth-, and sixth-graders, acting out highlights in the history of Royston. On cleanup day, 140 students appeared. They swept sidewalks, cleared alleys, and washed storefronts. They pulled weeds and planted flowers. Teachers rolled up their sleeves, too. So did merchants, store employees, and even onlookers who found themselves drawn into a community effort the likes of which Royston had never seen before.

In the middle of this activity were the two old buildings. Gerald Carey had given the kids permission to start ripping down loose shingles. Inside one building, Carey himself was at work with a crew. "Hello, Mr. Carey," the RIPPLES students hollered, happy to see "their" buildings being renovated. The student with the biggest grin was Matt Wilson, who could recognize his drawings coming to life.

On May 22, 1985, the last day of school, the sixth-graders and their teacher sat around the same table where they had first discussed the plan to revitalize their town. By now a discount drugstore chain had looked at the city council's survey and decided to open a store in Royston. A supermarket chain was also coming.

"What did you learn from all this?" Alice Terry asked.

"That you have to care enough to do something," replied Julinna.

Today the two restored buildings are the home of a new clothing store. Though still not a boomtown, Royston has begun to come back to life. City planners have written an optimistic master plan for further development. Royston has become a town with a future. Says Chamber of Commerce president Greg Hall: "Before RIPPLES we had little growth in five years. Now we have over twenty new businesses. Our town has more potential than ever."

On September 26, 1986, Alice Terry and her students walked on stage in a large auditorium in Washington, D.C., before 300 spectators. Donald P. Hodel, Secretary of the Interior, read a proclamation:

> "This group of perceptive, energetic young people proved the educational system can make a dynamic contribution to the preservation movement and inspire the teamwork necessary to promote change. For their creativity, ingenuity, and perseverance, Brandee Braswell, Derrick Gable, Judi Gurley, Julinna Oxley, and Matt Wilson of RIPPLES, and their inspiring instructor, Alice Terry, are granted the Public Service Award of the Department of the Interior."

When the applause and standing ovation came, so did Alice Terry's tears. Surrounded by her students, she knew: Every one of us can make a difference. Kids, too. We only have to try.

What Is Service-Learning?

According to Colin Powell, founding chairman of America's Promise,

> Service-learning is a particularly fertile way of involving young people in community service, because it ties helping others to what they are learning in the classroom. In the process, it provides a compelling answer to the perennial question: "Why do I need to learn this stuff?" (Fiske 2002, 2)

Arising from a heritage of service in America, service-learning provides students with an opportunity for service while putting them directly in the midst of the learning process. Service-learning emerged from the ideas of John Dewey who promoted active, real-world learning. A critic of rote learning of facts in schools, Dewey argued that children should learn by experience; in this way, he contended, students not only gain knowledge but also develop skills, habits, and attitudes necessary for them to solve a wide variety of problems (Dewey 1954).

Service-learning is a method by which students learn and develop through curriculum integration and active participation in thoughtfully organized service experiences that address actual needs in their community. It gives opportunities for students to use newly acquired skills and knowledge in real-life situations in their own communities. (National and Community Service Act 1990).

Acknowledging service-learning as a proven method of instruction that enhances learning and reclaims the public purpose of education, the National Commission on Service-Learning has recommended that quality service-learning be required as an essential part of K–12 education for all students in America. According to Madeleine Kunin, former deputy secretary of the U.S. Department of Education, "Service-learning resurrects idealism, compassion and altruism . . . [W]e cannot survive as a nation unless we hold onto these qualities and teach them to our children" (Fiske 2002, 38). This statement exemplifies the new realization of the importance of service-learning in instilling the qualities of a caring society in the leaders of tomorrow.

Some educators fear that service-learning may be just another add-on in an already-overcrowded school agenda. Service-learning, however, is an effective partner with the majority of school-reform initiatives. The American Youth Policy Forum investigated the applicability of service-learning to twenty-eight of the leading comprehensive school reform models. In twenty-four of the twenty-eight cases, service-learning was rated as compatible with the school-reform models; eleven of the twenty-four rated themselves as highly compatible with service-learning (Pearson 2002). In this time of federal budget cuts for many educational programs, liberal and conservative politicians alike have continued to support service-learning. Teachers can apply for Learn and Serve America grants (see "Service-Learning Resources" in Appendix B) to support their service-learning projects through their state education departments.

What Does the Service *in Service-Learning Mean?*

Just what does service mean? Though it may seem to be a simple term, service in reference to service-learning can be confusing because it is used in connection with many other terms. In service-learning, service is usually defined as the action(s) taken by youth to address a community issue in a positive manner. The students themselves are known as the service providers while those receiving the service are called the service recipients. In this book, we are looking at service through the lens of the service provider—the students. What are the students doing and how are they doing it?

Types of Service

We postulate that there are two basic types of service in reference to the service provider: direct service and indirect service. We have identified three types of direct service—*hands-on* service, *advocacy* service, and *secondhand* service. In *hands-on service*, students take positive, hands-on action to make a difference in the community through needed projects that are identified, organized, and implemented by the students. Students performing *advocacy service* engage in social action and advocacy designed to impact decision making on public issues by raising public awareness, working to get bills passed, and so on. Students can also choose to become involved in *secondhand service* by working to assist and support existing, established efforts such as the Cancer Society, Kidney Foundation, Save the Rain Forest, MADD, Just Say No, or Meals on Wheels.

Students can select one type of direct service that can be used for the duration of the service-learning experience, or a team can commingle their approach. More advanced levels of service-learning might involve students choosing to overlap more than one type of direct service within the same service-learning activity. As the students become more involved in and committed to a community concern, they may uncover aspects of the problem that suggest a new approach; hence, different types of direct service might be employed within the same service-learning experience.

Indirect service from the perspective of the service provider and the community refers to service that may not be seen immediately, and sometimes not for many years to come. For instance, indirect service could include cases where students through their service-learning participation become exposed to future career choices that they wouldn't otherwise have known about, or when, long after a service-learning project is over, students, as adults, exercise their right to vote. When viewing a service experience through the lens of indirect service, the community can be considered the service recipient.

Why Is Service-Learning Important for Adolescent Students?

Service-learning is important for middle- and high-school students because adolescents need to be involved in learning that they consider relevant—something that interests them. Most adolescents are curious, wondering about themselves and the world around them. They are consumed with questions such as Who am I?, Where am I going?, and What's it all about? (Conrad and Hedin 1991). These adolescents must be given the opportunity to find out how they fit into the larger world outside of school as well as the opportunity to express themselves positively in real-world situations. They must learn skills so they can become more responsive and effective citizens and become more confident and compassionate human beings. By gaining *passion* for their community, students develop *compassion* themselves.

Adolescence can be considered a time of great developmental transition. Early adolescence is characterized by substantial growth and change. In the United States, adolescence now extends over so many years that it can be divided into three phases: early adolescence, from ten to fourteen; middle adolescence, from fifteen to seventeen; and late adolescence, from eighteen into the twenties (Carnegie Council on Adolescent Development 1989).

If we are to believe developmental psychologists such as Piaget, Bandura, Kohlberg, and Gilligan, then development rather than achievement should be the aim of education. Shouldn't education help young adolescents in their search for identity? If so, service-learning is a marvelous method of learning as it deals with real-life experiences, something that is meaningful to the adolescent himself.

Recent reports and school-reform proposals point out the benefits to adolescents involved in service to their community, acknowledging the fit between the characteristics of this age group and active learning. In addition to addressing many traditional goals of the middle school, service-learning also is uniquely responsive to the traits of adolescents. These traits include the need to test oneself, to experience adult roles, to experiment with new relationships, to be trusted, and to cross the bridge from school and family into the community—the world beyond (Schine 1996). In service-learning, the learning is meaningful to the students. As one student involved in a service-learning project related, "I've learned skills that I think are more important than what you learn in school: like problem solving, organization skills, and teamwork" (Bohnenberger and Terry 2002, 6).

Adolescence is a critical period of both biological and psychological changes for middle- and high-school students. There is a critical need to help adolescents acquire self-esteem, flexible and inquiring habits of mind, reliable, close human relationships, a sense of belonging to a valued group, and a sense of usefulness that extends beyond themselves (Carnegie Council on Adolescent Development 1989). Because puberty is one of the most far-reaching biological upheavals in life, involving drastic changes in the social environment as young adolescents move from elementary to secondary schools, we need to connect schools with communities that together share responsibility for each student's success. This step can be done through identifying service opportunities in the community, establishing partnerships and collaborations, and using community resources to enrich the instructional program.

Service-learning fascinates young adolescents because it appeals to their idealism and quest for independence. They have ideal notions of what families, schools, churches, and societies ought to look like; they are known to rebel against the imperfect ones they experience. Not understanding why the rest of the world does not accept their idealistic solutions to social problems, they may become angry and destructive. Service-learning provides these idealistic youths with creative and useful means to try out new solutions so they can realize that they can indeed make a difference in the real world.

Middle schools and high schools, through the establishment of small learning communities (see Chapter 6), can provide favorable environments in which to create a culture of service that truly link service and learning and that encourage teacher-student collaboration to meet the educational and developmental needs of students. According to Bill Gates (Gates 2005), the new 3Rs of education, which have replaced reading, 'riting, and 'rithmetic are Rigor, Relevance, and Relationships. Gates, who with his wife, Melinda, has been instrumental in encouraging the development of small learning communities through the Bill and Melinda Gates Foundation, defined the 3Rs in a speech to the National Governors Association.

> The first R is Rigor—making sure all students are given challenging curriculum that prepares them for college and work; the second R is Relevance—making sure kids have courses and projects that clearly relate to their lives and goals; the third R is Relationships—making sure that kids have a number of adults who know them, look out for them, and push them to achieve. (Gates 2005, 4)

Service-learning has the potential of being especially strong in small learning community school environments because these environments promote experimentation, risk taking, challenging curriculum, collegiality, cooperation, and shared leadership among administrators, teachers, and students.

The power of service-learning is that it is a path to learning for adolescents; it places them in a context in which the learning is real, having consequences for both themselves and others. Judith A. Ramaley, assistant director of the National Science Foundation's Directorate for Education and Human Resources, expressed the importance of engaging students in real-world, service-learning experiences:

> If we want our students to lead creative, productive lives, we must give them opportunities to learn in ways that have consequences for

others, as well as for themselves. I know of no better way to invoke the many facets of cognitive development, moral reasoning and social responsibility than to engage students in service-learning opportunities. At its best, a service-learning experience can be transformative. (Fiske 2002, 58)

What Is Meant by Community in Service-Learning?

Although *community* can be defined as local, state, national, or global, effective service-learning activities usually center on a local need area, one with which the students can readily identify and have more of an impact upon. By identifying a local concern and learning to work cooperatively in teams toward a common goal, the students learn to manage people, projects, and their time. They begin to see a *purpose* for their education and develop a personal commitment both to learning and to their local community. This action-based, hands-on mode of learning and teaching turns the classroom into an authentic learning community that bridges the gap between school and the *real* world. It promotes the student's sense of responsibility to self and community.

Benefits to the Community from Service-Learning

The community experiences both direct and indirect benefits when students participate in service-learning. The most obvious benefits are direct ones, when students tackle a community problem and bring about a difference-making solution. In the previously mentioned story of the RIPPLES Gang, it's easy to see how the students had a positive impact on their town. Service-learning, as this example illustrates, establishes a positive rapport between the community and the school. The actual value of the service to a community depends upon the issue the students identify and select as the focus of their service-learning project. Obviously, each community will have different need areas.

Some benefits to the community may not be evident in the short term but are important to the community in the long term. These indirect benefits can include students becoming more engaged in school and furthering their education; youth becoming resources rather than responsibilities and/or problems in a society; and young people evolving into responsible, participatory citizens.

Are There Different Types of Service-Learning?

Many different types of service-learning activities are often grouped together under the service-learning umbrella. This consolidation has often led to confusion for educators trying to develop effective programming for their students as well as for evaluators trying to assess program impacts and outcomes. Service-learning is not an easily definable activity, and comparing one type of service-learning experience to another can be like comparing apples to oranges. Apples and oranges are both fruit, but they don't look, smell, or taste the same. It is the same with service-learning: results from fifth graders who participate in a service-learning experience that involves the students volunteering at a local park or recreation area to clean up litter and fallen brush should not be mixed with results from ninth graders who research environmentally friendly land-use options in their community and work with community partners to develop an action plan to design, build, and maintain a community nature trail or habitat. Both are environmental projects that resulted in worthwhile service to the community, but they shouldn't be classified as the same type of service-learning.

The developmental service-learning typology created by the authors (see chart in Appendix B) addresses the differences between service-learning activities based on the levels of both student learning and service. Using this typology, teachers can help their students progress from simple community-service activities in their younger years to more involved projects as they become more experienced in serving and learning. By classifying service-learning according to the impact on student learning and both the type and degree of service to the community, this typology provides a much-needed basic framework for educators, evaluators, and administrators. It distinguishes between three levels of service-learning—Community-Service, Community-Exploration, and Community-Action.

Developmental Service-Learning Typology

Like a thermometer, the service-learning degrees, or levels of involvement, work on a continuum, as shown in Figure 1–1, rather than on sharply delineated points.

Community-Service (see Chapter 2) involves a high degree of service with a lesser degree of learning. The interaction between the school and community flows in one direction—from the school to the community. Students sometimes participate in Community-Service to complete a specified number of volunteer hours in order to meet designated service requirements. Some service-learning advocates question whether this type of volunteerism should even be considered "service-learning." When using a developmental model, community-service is appropriate as an entry-level experience, especially for less mature students who have never participated in service-learning or

Figure 1–1

Learning Arrows: directional arrows signifying the degree of learning—increasing as they move toward the pinnacle.

Service Circles: illustrate the extent of direct service to the community by the student.

Side Arrows: symbolize the flow of interaction between the community and the school.

Thermometer: a continuum depicting the degree of the combined service and learning experience.

for students operating at a lower cognitive developmental stage. This type of direct service can include the following:

- Activities such as picking up litter in town parks or on the side of highways, shelving books in the library, volunteering in a hospital or nursing home, cleaning up graffiti, or donating time on a school or community "hotline."

- Students collecting service hours by volunteering time to aid non-profit agencies.

Participation in Community-Service usually increases an aware-ness of community needs and leads to curriculum- and service-specific learning for the student. Higher degrees of reflection and a stronger connection to the curriculum lead to increased student learning.

Community-Exploration (see Chapter 3) directly connects class-room learning to real-life situations. Many schools incorporate service-learning into the curriculum through classes such as civics, art, science, history, health, language arts, reading, or computer technol-ogy. Community-Exploration involves tying the student service to an activity related to a specific area of study; it can involve intern-ships, community information-gathering, environmental education, and other types of experiential education. Interaction between the school and community can flow in either direction—students go out into the community or elements of the community can come into the school. Community-Exploration does not necessarily involve di-rect service to the community, although it may involve a high degree of learning.

Community-Action (see Chapter 4) involves students not only be-coming aware of a need in the community and providing a service but also becoming so involved and committed to the need area that they go beyond just supplying a service. Students analyze the situation, generate new ideas, and implement a difference-making plan of ac-tion. In the process, the students develop complex problem solving skills, advanced communication skills, the ability to connect knowl-edge across the disciplines, and the perseverance to overcome obsta-cles. In Community-Action service-learning, the interaction between the school and the community flows in both directions, producing greater impact in the community and greater empowerment in the students. Community-Action projects foster the highest degree of ser-vice and learning and have far-reaching outcomes in the community. In the case of the RIPPLES Gang, their Community-Action project led to the restoration of two historic buildings, a professional market study for their community, and a massive cleanup and revitalization of their downtown.

Getting Started in Service-Learning

You must consider a number of things when selecting and planning the level of service-learning that would work best for you and your students. First, confer with your colleagues to ascertain the options and support for service-learning in your school or system. It is important to find out if and how service-learning is currently facilitated.

- Is service-learning recommended or required in your school?
- Are students required to attain a specific number of service hours?
- Must the actual service take place during school time?
- Is there administrative support for service-learning to be integrated into the curriculum?
- Will the service-learning activity need cross-department planning?
- Is there a school or community service-learning coordinator available for input or assistance?
- Is service-learning congruent with the mission statement of your school?
- How much time do you plan to devote to service-learning as a part of your curriculum?

Because you must not view service-learning as an add-on to any curriculum but as a pedagogy for teaching curriculum standards, start with your curriculum standards as you begin service-learning. Although not pointing to any specific curriculum objectives, as they vary by content and location, we have identified possible curricular connections (CC) in Chapters 2, 3, and 4 (see "Starter Ideas" in Chapters 2, 3, and 4).

After you have identified your curriculum standards and how you will integrate service-learning into your curriculum, you should determine the level of service-learning that is most appropriate for your students and school situation. Carefully examine the Developmental Service-Learning Typology (see chart in Appendix B) and its accompanying table on types of service-learning. The typology is correlated to Piaget's cognitive developmental stages, Bloom's Taxonomy, and Bradley's levels of reflection. The typology table outlines the activities, effects, and best practices at all three levels of service-learning. This information will help you establish the level of service-learning for which your students are developmentally ready.

A brief example of how the curriculum connection might differ depending on the level of service-learning chosen follows.

If your students are working at the Community-Service level and volunteering service hours, you might want to limit their volunteer options to needs specific to your curriculum. For instance, if you are teaching a unit on water pollution, students could participate in cleaning up trash or debris on a local streambed or riverbank. Be sure to extend their learning by connecting their service to the unit content through appropriate reflective activities.

In the same type of unit at the Community-Exploration level, you might want the students to investigate the types and causes of water pollution in your city, learn how to test the water quality, and visit a local water-treatment facility or invite an expert in the field to talk to your class. The students can then write a report and reflect on their findings.

At the Community-Action level, the additional activities might include testing the local waterways and water storage facilities for the presence of pollutants. If pollutants are found, the students could devise and implement a plan of action designed to reduce the water pollution.

What Are the Logistics Involved in Service-Learning?

So how are you going to organize this thing called service-learning? We wish we could give you a simple outline. That is not possible, however, because each service-learning experience and each teacher are different. This is the exciting part of service-learning! You get to organize your service-learning experience to suit your style of teaching and your classroom needs and limitations. You can do service-learning to fit your schedule and curriculum. You can do it daily, once a week, one week a month, after school, on weekends—whenever you like! Everything depends on the focus of your service-learning experience and how you will incorporate it into your curriculum. Will it be an integral part of your curriculum or an add-on? If it is an add-on, you might want to use differentiation strategies such as compacting the curriculum. Using this approach, you could plan to do service-learning one day a week; Fridays are ideal for participating in service-learning after you have covered all your weekly objectives. Much depends on the type of service-learning you do as well. Whereas a Community-Action service-learning experience might consume more time, a Community-Service service-learning experience might take only a day or a week to complete. It all depends on the service-learning experience you and your students undertake. That is the beauty of service-learning. Unlike some programs that are scripted, service-learning can be fashioned to meet your needs and those of your students. See Chapter 5, "Implementing Service-Learning in the Classroom," for more ideas and suggestions.

Basic Ingredients for Service-Learning

The basic components of service-learning follow:

1. Preparation—the groundwork for identifying and preparing for the service-learning experience.
2. Action—carrying out the service-learning experience.

3. Reflection—analyzing, processing, synthesizing, and evaluating the information and ideas encountered during the service-learning experience.

4. Celebration—acknowledging, honoring, and validating the students' service-learning effort.

Preparation—Getting Started in Service-Learning *Preparation* is, simply put, getting started in the service-learning experience. It is making important decisions, such as how the experience will be carried out. Will it be in your classroom? After school? Will it involve all your students? Only volunteers? Will students receive credit of some sort? What is the focus of the service? Will you be doing Community-Service, Community-Exploration, or Community-Action service-learning? Who might work with you on the project? Any community partners? Have you gotten your administration to support the endeavor?

Ready, Set, Go! Carrying Out the Action So you've decided what to do and are ready to start your service-learning experience. How you proceed with the action will depend on what type of service-learning you have chosen: Community-Service, Community-Exploration, or Community-Action. Action ideas and best-practice models for each level of service-learning are discussed in detail in Chapters 2, 3 and 4.

Reflection—The Learning Element In education, more value is usually accorded to service-learning activities that result in more academic learning by the students. An effective way to promote learning in service-learning activities is through the use of reflection. *Reflection* is an essential part of service-learning; it is the process of looking back on actions taken to determine what has been gained, lost, or achieved and connecting these results to future actions and larger societal contexts. Reflection utilizes creative and critical thinking processes to help youth convert their service experience into a productive learning experience (Alliance for Service-Learning in Education Reform 1993).

Reflection is the framework through which students process and synthesize the information and ideas they have gained through their service-learning experiences. Through the process of reflection, students analyze concepts, examine and evaluate their experiences, and form their own opinions (Alliance for Service-Learning in Education Reform 1993).

The three levels of reflection follow:

- Level One: *Observation*—recognition of a dilemma.
- Level Two: *Analysis*—responding, framing, and reframing.
- Level Three: *Synthesis*—use of experimentation and strategy selection (Bradley 1995).

Although extremely important in establishing the learning aspect of service-learning, reflection is unfortunately often pushed aside due to time constraints. Chapters 2, 3, and 4 explain how the levels of reflection correspond to each service-learning level—Community-Service, Community-Exploration, and Community-Action. These chapters also include a suggested list of reflective activities at each level.

Celebration—Enhancing the Experience for Students Celebration is an important component of service-learning whereby the good work the students have done is acknowledged. From a simple recognition certificate or a party to formal recognition by the town council or state legislature, celebration enhances service-learning experiences for youth by validating their efforts and honoring their contributions.

In order to gain the most from their service-learning experiences, students need exposure to the 3Rs of celebration: Recognition, Reward, and Respect. Celebratory activities can range from teachers arranging a pizza or ice cream party in class or at a local pizza or ice cream parlor within walking distance to showing a movie after school with snacks or holding a skating party or cookout on a Saturday. In addition to these fun activities to honor the students' work, businesses, clubs, organizations, and government agencies often recognize the efforts made by students to improve their communities. This recognition can range from the awarding of certificates and trophies to the presenting of cash prizes or scholarships for individual or group efforts. Exemplary service-learning experiences can sometimes gain national recognition for the students and their school (see "Opportunities for Celebration and Demonstration" in Appendix B).

Using Choice and Voice to Identify a Need Area

Giving the students a *choice* and *voice* in determining the focus for the service-learning activity helps to ensure at least some degree of interest from the onset of the service-learning experience. As the students proceed through the service-learning activities and become empowered to make an actual difference in their community, their interest level soars. Keeping the curriculum and student learning objectives in mind, you might want to compile a list of possibilities for the students to choose from as a class. Chapters 2, 3, and 4 contain examples of possible service-learning activities at each level of involvement—Community-Service, Community-Exploration, and Community-Action.

At the Community-Exploration and Community-Action levels, after the students have brainstormed, discussed, and decided on the top two or three options, you can divide the class into groups and have each group research a different option. Their assignment would be to find out how much of a problem the selected concern actually is in their community and to report their findings to the class (see Chapter 5). This research might take the form of interviewing schoolmates or town residents, checking the current and back issues of the local newspaper, and gaining insight into the general problem area by researching the topic in the library or on the Internet and then connecting it to the concern in their community.

If possible, the students should take an Awareness Walk to the actual site for investigative purposes. If the students are unable to actually walk through the area, try to arrange a time for them to make observations through the windows of a car or school bus. It is important for later planning purposes that the students have firsthand knowledge of how the problem affects their community.

Assessment in Service-Learning

How do you assess your students in service-learning? Since service-learning is a pedagogy just like group work or lecture, you would assess your content objectives in the same manner you would for other topics. For instance, if your content involves history objectives, you would assess your students' knowledge of the subject matter using the same method you would normally use, be it essay, multiple-choice, or short-answer tests.

So how would you assess the students' service-learning involvement? You could both assess and promote student learning through reflective activities, informal, formal, or both. Actually the use of both measures is ideal. Using formative and summative assessments serves to increase student learning concerning the service-learning experience. During the service-learning experience, students should be given opportunities to reflect on the meaning of the experience. Formative assessment could involve informal assessment where you ask the students to discuss their ideas and feelings in an informal setting. Perhaps you set aside a few minutes at the end of class for the students to share and discuss their ideas and insights from the experience. Students could also journal their ideas and feelings on a regular basis. Journaling is an effective tool for reflection for students. Summative assessment could also be informal or formal. At the end of the experience, a summative assessment captures the essence of the experience for the students. What did they take away from the experience? What impact has it had or will it have on them? On the community? This approach can include techniques such as discussion, journaling, a project, or a paper. Chapters 2, 3, and 4 offer level-specific suggestions for reflection. Specific techniques and tools for assessment can be found in Chapter 5 and in Appendix A.

Ask the Experts

Chapters 1 through 4 contain an *Ask the Experts* section at the end of each chapter that contains questions relevant to service-learning in general and the service-learning typology specifically. Chapter 1 questions follow:

1. *Why is a developmental service-learning typology needed?*

In order to implement and sustain service-learning in elementary and secondary schools, teachers need to understand what service-learning entails. So often, all we give them is the PARC model: Preparation, Action, Reflection, and Celebration. Then we parade wonderful examples of high-quality service-learning projects students have been involved in. We have found that this method can be overwhelming to teachers and can turn them away from service-learning altogether. This typology provides not only a developmental model but one that can help teachers determine the best type of service-learning for their students based on what is appropriate for their students, the content objectives for their course, and the amount of time they have to dedicate to service-learning.

2. *I know of a high school that had a school culture troubled with disrespect and violence between poor white students (half the population) and Native American students (the other half). The school instituted a program of service work in the community where the students from the two cultures worked together on a team. There was much time dedicated to the planning and discussion of the teamwork, and the school culture was transformed by the teamwork and discussion groups. Which level of your typology would this project fit into?*

The way the question is worded makes it difficult to determine into which level this project fits. If the high school officials developed and instituted the program as is implied in the question, and there is no service being done by the students when they are in groups together, in addition to not having any reflection during the experience by the students as well as a lack of connection to the curriculum, then perhaps it isn't service-learning at all, even though it sounds like a wonderful program that obviously made a difference in the school culture. However, if the students themselves developed and instituted the program through research and problem solving and did synthesis-level reflection during the experience, and the project connected to some part of their curriculum, then it could be a Community-Action service-learning experience. If the school officials themselves developed and instituted the program and the students just worked in groups doing service together (such as picking up trash in the community or cleaning up graffiti) and did observation-level reflection with adequate ties to the curriculum, it would slot into Community-Service

service-learning. If the students did higher-level reflections involving analysis, it would slot into Community-Exploration (the higher the level of reflection, the higher degree on the service-learning thermometer). If, seeing how powerful the program was at the high school, the students themselves created and implemented a similar program in the middle school, then it would advance to Community-Action with appropriate levels of reflection and connections to the curriculum. (Note: this type of experience could easily be connected to curriculum objectives in civics and character education. It is important, however, that there be a connection to the curriculum; otherwise, it just becomes a project that after-school service groups like Key Club or Tri-Hi-Y might carry out.)

3. *How does giving students choice and voice factor into the different levels of service-learning?*

The more *choice* and *voice* you give students, the greater their commitment to their service-learning experience. Giving the students more voice means that they will be more instrumental in determining the course of the service-learning experience, which can demand a higher level of cognition. In that students are taking action and using advanced problem solving skills in Community-Action service-learning, you can conclude generally that the more *choice* and *voice* you give students, the higher the degree the experience will be on the service-learning typology.

4. *What is the difference between assessment and reflection?*

Reflection is the key to meaningful service-learning. In service-learning, reflection promotes—possibly even provides—much of the learning. Although teachers can use a traditional assessment instrument for some of the content objectives, assessing the learning from the service is not that simple. The students need to be prompted to reflect on their experience and what it means. As in most experiential learning, this reflection can be performed through class or group discussions, journaling, drawing, or writing such as poetry. How the teacher assesses the reflections is completely left to him or her, as it should be. We see assessment of the service as a help to the teacher in directing the service-learning further. If students are confused about some aspect of the service, reflective activities provide opportunities for teachers to get at that confusion and clear up any misunderstandings. For instance, if students are involved through their service-learning experience with the Red Cross and confuse this nonprofit organization with government agencies, this confusion can surface during reflective activities. Teachers could use rubrics to assess the reflective writing. If this is a language arts class and writing components are assessed in the reflections, use of a rubric is appropriate. If, however, levels of reflection are being assessed, teachers must be cautious and use the developmentally-appropriate rubric. Some students may not be ready developmentally to reflect at the higher levels of analysis or synthesis. Following the guidelines for reflection offered in this book should be helpful.

References

Alliance for Service Learning in Education Reform. 1993. "Standards of Quality and Excellence for School-Based Learning." Washington, DC: Council of Chief State School Officers.

Bohnenberger, Jann, and Alice W. Terry. 2002. "Community Problem Solving Works for Middle Level Students." *Middle School Journal* 34 (1): 5–12.

Bradley, James. 1995. "A Model for Evaluating Student Learning in Academically Based Service." In *Connecting Cognition and Action: Evaluation of Student Performance in Service Learning Courses*, edited by M. Troppe, 13–26. Providence, RI: Campus Compact.

Carnegie Council on Adolescent Development. 1989. *Turning Points: Preparing American Youth for the 21st Century*. New York: Carnegie Corporation of New York.

Conrad, Dan, and Diane Hedin. 1991. "Service: A Pathway to Knowledge." *Journal of Cooperative Education* 27 (2): 73–84.

Dewey, John. 1954. *The Public and Its Problems*. Athens, OH: Swallow Press.

Fiske, Edward B. 2002. "Learning in Deed: The Power of Service-Learning for American Schools." Newton, MA: National Commission on Service-Learning.

Gates, Bill. 2005. "Keynote Address." In *National Summit on High Schools*. Washington, DC, 4.

Henderson, Bruce. 1987. "The Kids Who Saved a Dying Town." *Reader's Digest*, September, 42–46.

National and Community Service Act of 1990. 1991. Pub. L. No. 101-610, 42 USC 12401; 104 Stat. 3127.

Pearson, Sarah. 2002. *"Finding Common Ground: Service-Learning and Education Reform: A Survey of 28 Leading School Reform Models."* Washington, DC: American Youth Policy Forum.

Schine, Joan. 1996. "Service Learning: A Promising Strategy for Connecting Students to Communities." *Middle School Journal* 28 (2): 3–9.

Standards of Quality for School-Based Service-Learning. 1995. In, ed. Alliance for Service-Learning in Education Reform. Close Up Foundation, http:// servicelearning.org/lib_svcs/bibs/cb_bibs/sl_glance/index.php?search_ term="Standards%20of%20quality%20for%20school-based%20and% 20community-based%20service-learning (accessed May 19, 2006).

Chapter Two

Community-Service
Service-Learning

The "Detour—Road Closed" signs went up on Royston's main streets the afternoon of May 15, 1985. Traffic was diverted as a horde of children descended on the downtown area. Their mission: to clean up the city's cluttered streets.

When the idea of a work detail was first discussed, one of Alice's fellow teachers scoffed, "No kid is going to volunteer for cleanup work." But the RIPPLES talked up the project and presented a skit to fourth-, fifth-, and sixth-graders, acting out highlights in the history of Royston. On cleanup day, 140 students appeared. They swept sidewalks, cleared alleys, and washed storefronts. They pulled weeds and planted flowers. Teachers rolled up their sleeves, too. So did merchants, store employees, and even onlookers who found themselves drawn into a community effort the likes of which Royston had never seen before. (Henderson 1987, 45)

Introduction

The RIPPLES Gang was shocked at how many students volunteered to help out—so many volunteered for this Community-Service (CS) service-learning experience that not all of them could go downtown; some had to remain at the school, cleaning up the playground. Although the RIPPLES Gang itself was actually participating at a higher level of service-learning when the group performed the history of Royston skit, discussed Royston's interesting history with other students in the school, and planned the massive schoolwide cleanup

Figure 2–1
Interaction between the school and the community goes one way—
from the school to the community.

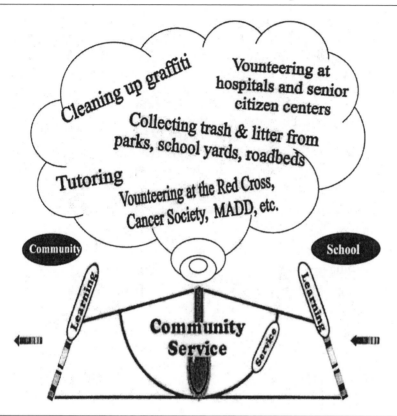

effort, the other students who learned about the need from the RIP-
PLES Gang and volunteered on Cleanup Day were participating at the
Community-Service level of service-learning.

Community-Service service-learning entails students volunteering in
their community and increasing their awareness of the community.
The term *community-service* is often associated with volunteerism, with
students completing a specified number of volunteer hours in order to
meet a designated number of service hours either for school graduation or judicatory requirements. Because of this, the hyphen between
Community and *Service* is added to differentiate it from what is tradi-
tionally considered community service—an activity that serves the

community but is not connected to the school curriculum. Teachers may choose to connect Community-Service service-learning to a curriculum goal by providing the students with volunteer choices specific to the curriculum or by promoting civic competence and character education objectives.

When taking a developmental approach to service-learning, beginning at the Community-Service level is appropriate for less mature students who have never participated in service-learning or for students operating at a lower cognitive developmental stage. Community-Service can be an important building block in establishing a foundation on which to build the skills necessary for students to eventually advance to higher levels of service-learning.

Usually involving a high degree of service with a lesser degree of learning, Community-Service can include *direct, hands-on* service activities such as:

- picking up litter in town parks or on the side of highways
- shelving books in the library
- volunteering in a hospital or nursing home
- cleaning up graffiti
- helping to build houses with Habitat for Humanity
- donating time on a school or community hotline

In addition to these activities, students may collect service hours by *direct*, secondhand service, which involves volunteering time to aid nonprofit agencies. Direct, second-hand service can include raising money or goods for already-existing organizations such as:

- The Kidney Foundation
- The Cancer Society
- MADD (Mothers Against Drunk Driving)
- Just Say No
- Special Olympics
- Meals on Wheels
- March of Dimes
- Save the Rainforest

In Community-Service service-learning, the interaction between the students and the community flows in one direction—from the students or the school to the community being served. Participation in Community-Service service-learning usually increases an awareness of community needs and leads to curriculum- and service-specific learning for the youth. The more reflection, the greater the learning.

Figure 2–2

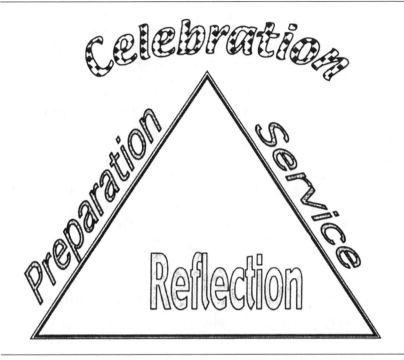

Best-Practice Model for Community-Service Service-Learning

This Community-Service service-learning model is the standard experiential education and service-learning model, which includes preparation, action, reflection, and celebration (see Chapter 1). Preparation is the first step in this model. During this step, the teacher can offer students a variety of service options that connect to the content area or have the students brainstorm and choose the actual service themselves. Next the teacher collaborates with community partners to plan the time and place for community-service activities. Action (Service) is the next step in this model. During this step, meaningful service is carried out by the students using both previous and acquired academic skills and knowledge. Reflection is the next step in this Community-Service service-learning model. Students are guided in their examination of the service experience at the Observation level of reflection. The final step in this model is Celebration. During this step, student work is acknowledged and validated.

Logistics of Community-Service

In Community-Service service-learning, the students usually go off campus to perform the service activity. There are times, however, when the students may elect to perform service activities such as picking up trash in the school yard, planting flowers or shrubs, or collecting used paper from the classrooms for recycling. In both cases, the teacher must plan when the community-service will take place and coordinate the effort with whomever will be the service recipient. If the service doesn't take place on the school campus, the teacher should secure administrative and parental permission for a field trip as well as work out transportation needs. The students may be able to walk to the site, but it is more likely that bus or car transportation must be secured and approved. Depending on the nature of the community-service activity and the number of students involved, the teacher may also need to arrange for chaperones to help oversee the students as they carry out their service experience.

Community-Service and Cognitive Development

Referencing Piaget's (1950) cognitive developmental stages, Community-Service service-learning corresponds to Piaget's third stage of cognitive development, the concrete operational stage. Participating primarily in volunteerism, students perceive issues that are individual rather than societal reflecting their link to the concrete world. Issues of society involve more abstract levels of reasoning, which can be difficult for students at this developmental stage to comprehend.

Community-Service and Critical Thinking

This typology has been correlated to Bloom's Taxonomy (1956) and Webb's Depth of Knowledge (1999). Community-Service service-learning corresponds to the first two levels of Bloom's Taxonomy, Knowledge and Comprehension. It corresponds to Webb's first level, recall. In Community-Service service-learning, students recall facts, terms. and basic concepts as well as demonstrate an understanding of facts and ideas by organizing, comparing, translating, interpreting, and stating main ideas. Participating in their service-learning experience, students might attempt to answer questions such as:

- What have you observed about this community situation?
- How, when, and why did this need develop?

- What service did you provide?
- Who were the main participants? List the service provider, service recipient, and community partner.
- How would you summarize the results of your service-learning experience?

Reflection During Community-Service

In Community-Service service-learning, the type of reflection carried out by the students is termed *Observation*. At the Observation level, reflection is usually informal with the students giving examples of observed behaviors, although the observations tend to be one-dimensional and focus on only one aspect of the situation (Bradley 1995). At this level, youth:

- Share general observations about their experience but do not necessarily provide an understanding of the reasons behind what they observed.
- Focus their reflections on what they observed during the service experience and/or discussed formally or informally without necessarily expanding on what was already said or incorporating it into the whole.
- Are likely to focus on more concrete aspects of the situation or area of concern.
- Employ both personal beliefs and established fact in their observations without recognizing a difference between the two.
- Recognize different points of view but are not necessarily aware of the differences between them.

Suggestions for Reflective Activities at the Community-Service (CS) level

- Students can write a brief weekly summary of the CS experience describing their observations.
- Students can discuss their experiences briefly during a class discussion period relating their observations.
- Students can draw something relating to their CS experience. It could be a person, a setting, or anything.
- Students can express their feelings about their CS experience through the use of poetry, drawing, painting, music, or dance.
- Students can role-play something they observed during the CS experience.

- Students can create a diorama dealing with some aspect of the CS experience.
- Students can write letters thanking someone involved in the CS activity, relating what they observed during the experience as well as their appreciation for the opportunity to be involved.
- Students can design a bulletin board in the classroom and/or the school that can be used to display photographs, drawings, writings, and so on.
- Students can create a scrapbook and/or portfolio of their activities.
- Students can design a webpage describing activities and experiences of the CS activities.
- Students can select digital photographs to use on a webpage to document the CS experience.

Starter Ideas for Community-Service Activities

The ideas that follow are intended to be a springboard in helping to connect service-learning both to your curriculum and to a concern in your community. After each activity, symbols have been added to denote a specific curriculum area connection (CC): LA represents language/arts; M represents math; SC represents science; SS represents social studies; A represents art; and CT represents computer technology.

- Create flyers or posters that explain where to vote in the next election and/or how to obtain absentee ballots (CC: LA, SS, A, CT).
- Make phone calls reminding people to vote and create list of those needing transportation to the polling place (CC: LA, SS).
- Volunteer in a cleanup, painting, or repair effort to help low-income or special-needs residents (CC: M, SS, A).
- Help elderly neighbors by mowing lawns, pulling weeds, emptying the trash, shoveling snow, or picking up items at the grocery store or pharmacy (CC: SC, SS).
- Volunteer with Habitat for Humanity (students must be at least sixteen years old) (CC: M, SS).
- Give walking tours of historical areas in the community (CC: LA, SS).
- Help in a community-beautification campaign by volunteering to pull weeds and plant flowers, shrubs, and trees (CC: SC, SS).
- Volunteer to work for a crime alert hotline (CC: LA, SS).

- Donate time as a helper or tour guide at a nature study center (CC: LA, SC, SS).
- Donate time as a helper or tour guide at an art museum (CC: LA, SS, A).
- Clear debris and groundcover to help create a community nature walk (CC: SC).
- Volunteer at city offices (CC: LA, SS, CT).
- Pick up and properly dispose of trash and debris from the side of the road, school yard, and parks (CC: SC).
- Volunteer at a public TV or radio station (CC: LA).
- Oversee a poster contest that promotes tolerance and understanding among different races, religions, and ethnic groups in the community (CC: LA, SS, A).
- Help to clean up and repair picnic tables, boat ramps, and recreational areas at parks (CC: LA, SC, SS).
- Recruit businesses to become safe places for children (CC: LA, SS).
- Be an art volunteer at a local daycare center or elementary school (CC: SS, A).
- Volunteer at the town or school library shelving books, working at the return counter, or helping locate books (CC: LA, SS).
- Visit with younger students and discuss the importance of education (CC: LA, SC, SS).
- Volunteer to work for a homework hotline in subjects in which the student excels (CC: LA, M, SC, or SS).
- Volunteer to tutor others in an area in which the student excels (CC: LA, M, SC, or SM).
- Make colorful math, science, or reading flash cards for younger students (CC: LA, M, SC, SA, or A).
- Hold a used-book sale and then donate the money to a literacy campaign (CC: LA, SS).
- Volunteer to read aloud to the visually impaired, learning disabled, and so on (CC: LA, SS).
- Collect and sort art and school supplies for children in need (CC: SS, A).
- Collect used books to be given to a library at a homeless shelter (CC: LA, SS).
- Donate time to teach computer skills to youth or adults in your community (CC: SS, CT).

- Volunteer time at a homeless shelter to tutor children on skills they may have missed (CC: LA, M, SC, or SS).
- Adopt an at-risk student as a learning buddy (CC: LA, M, SC, or SS).
- Volunteer time at community centers, preschools, or after-school care to read to children or play literacy games (CC: LA, SS).
- Volunteer after school or during a free period to work as a student aide in the school office or for a specific teacher (CC: SS, CT perhaps).
- Volunteer to meet and greet new students and help them become acclimated (CC: LA, SS).
- Serve on a peer mediation task force to help reduce conflicts and increase a positive climate for learning (CC: LA, SS).
- Volunteer time to repair used books and learning materials (CC: SS).
- Clean up a streambed or river bank (CC: SC, SS).
- Create a recycling plan for the school (CC: SC, SS).
- Volunteer to monitor recycling in each homeroom (CC: M, SS).
- Start an environmental club in your school to provide volunteer services (CC: SC, SS).
- Volunteer at a local parks and recreation areas (CC: SS).
- Serve on a crew to plant seedlings on Arbor Day and/or Earth Day (CC: SC, SS).
- Conduct energy audits of the school, students' homes, or city buildings (CC: M, SC, SS).
- Create and distribute flyers listing home recycling ideas (CC: SC, SS, A, CT).
- Volunteer at a nature habitat or zoo (CC: SC, SS).
- Volunteer at an environmental information booth in shopping malls, fairs, and so on (CC: SC, SS).
- Help to build a walking path at a local park (CC: SC, SS).
- Volunteer at the Audubon Society (CC: SC, SS).
- Present an environmental awareness program to children in after-school care or at community centers (CC: SC, SS).
- Volunteer to pull weeds and clean up the grounds for elderly or infirm residents (CC: SS).
- Create or monitor a website on which volunteers can sign up to participate in community cleanup activities; park, trail, and shoreline maintenance; water testing; or other *green* activities (CC: SC, SS).

- Serve as a youth representative on an environmental council or on a parks department or zoological gardens committee (CC: SC, SS).
- Create or update an environmental wish list for the community (CC: SC, SS).
- Set up or volunteer at a school composting area for cafeteria waste (CC: SC, SS).
- Help out with a blood drive (CC: SS).
- Volunteer at the Red Cross, Cancer Society, Kidney Foundation, MADD, the county health center, and so on (CC: SS).
- Volunteer for a hotline for those who need help finding available health resources (CC: SS).
- Volunteer at hospitals, rehabilitation centers, or health centers (CC: SS).
- Organize walkathons to increase awareness of various health needs (CC: SS).
- Volunteer at after-school centers to repair sports equipment or toys, help with outside activities, or teach classes on a sport in which the student excels (CC: SS).
- Help to raise money to buy smoke detectors for the homes without them (CC: SS).
- Hand out a home-safety checklist to all residents in your community (CC: SS).
- Volunteer at the Boy's or Girl's Club, YMCA, YWCA, or community centers that offer after-school care for children (CC: SS).
- Encourage people to sign organ donor cards by volunteering at an organ donor table at a shopping mall or local health fair (CC: SS).
- Collect pledges in the school for an antismoking campaign (CC: SS).
- Volunteer at churches or organizations that provide safe places for children and/or health training for the community (CC: SS).
- Volunteer at the Humane Society or local animal shelter (CC: SS).
- Serve as an animal handler in pet therapy sessions offered to nursing homes and hospitals (CC: SS).
- Read to seniors in a nursing home or hospital (CC: LA, SS).
- Use students' talents to entertain the elderly in nursing homes or veterans hospitals (CC: SS).
- Serve food in a homeless shelter or mission (CC: SS).
- Become a Meals on Wheels volunteer (CC: SS).

- Participate in a drive to collect food, clothing, or furniture for the needy (CC: SS).
- Pack and/or deliver holiday food baskets to the hungry (CC: SS).
- Work at a community garden representing an elderly or disabled person so he or she can receive a portion of the produce grown (CC: SS).
- Volunteer at a community center to teach basic skills to English as a Second Language (ESL) families (CC: SS).
- Create and/or distribute flyers to increase awareness of a community health clinic and its services (CC: SS).
- Sort clothes and/or work at a distribution center for the needy (CC: SS).
- Serve as a volunteer helper at the Special Olympics (CC: SS).

Examples of Community-Service Service-Learning

Adopt-A-Grandparent Project

The fourth-graders strolled downtown on a brisk fall afternoon with their teacher leading the way. To complement the student's lessons about the history of their town and its institutions, their teacher set up an Adopt-A-Grandparent service-learning project for them in partnership with the local nursing home. The first meeting with students and residents of the nursing home was a party with cake and balloons. The children met their adopted grandparents and thus began the relationship. The students could visit their "grandparent" on their own time, and some did. Otherwise the school's involvement was primarily through greeting cards and class discussions.

After the first meeting with the *grandparents*, the teacher held a class discussion. While the students sat in a circle on the floor surrounding the teacher, the teacher asked questions like: What did you observe about the nursing home? Describe the people who work there and the residents themselves. Tell the class about your grandparent. What did you talk to him/her about while you were there? Do you think the residents of the nursing home enjoyed the visit? Why? Why not?

Each holiday, the students worked on their writing skills by creating newsy greeting cards for their grandparents. The teacher then delivered the cards to the nursing home. The grandparents also sent letters to the children. Some children visited their grandparents on their own time after school hours, although they were not required to do so. In the art class, the students painted pictures about their experience, which were later hung on a bulletin board outside the art classroom.

The class discussed the project several times throughout the year. During the last week of school, the students trekked back to the nursing home with their teacher and some parent volunteers for a final visit with their grandparents. The social director for the nursing home planned another party for the group. When they returned to the school, the teacher had the students write thank-you cards to their grandparents. After completing the cards, the teacher directed the students to write an essay summarizing the experience. The students were asked to share their observations about the experience, their grandparents, and their feelings about the experience.

An example of a Community-Service reflection of the experience follows:

> I have a new grandmother. Her name is Cassie Smith and she lives at the Simpson Nursing Home. She has two children. One lives in town and comes to see her on Sunday most of the time. She has 3 grandchildren who come to see her sometimes and there is a picture of them by her bed. There [sic] names are Sandy, John, and Susie. Susie goes to the high school. She is a cheerleeder [sic].
>
> I call my new grandmother Nana Cass. That's what she says Sandy, John, and Susie call her. She smiles when I call her that. Nana Cass has been at the nursing home for 2 years. She is real sweet but she has a hard time getting around. She has a thing that helps her get around better. But she doesn't seem sad about it. She doesn't seem sad about anything.
>
> I sent her three cards and she has them up on her wall by the window. I think she likes them a lot. It makes me feel good to see them up like that, like I did something good. When I went back to see her yesterday she told the lady in the room with her I was the one who sent her those cards. She asked me if I was going to send her any more cards or come back to see her. I told her I was going to try and would come if my mom would bring me back. I want to see her again.
>
> I guess where Nana Cass lives is a good place but I don't think I would want to live there. They have a nice lady that does parties for them there. That was fun. It smells funny there though. It's not a bad smell but smells different. Nobody says anything about it so I don't either.
>
> I'm glad I got to do this and meet Nana Cass. She is sweet and likes to talk. She sent me a card too. I hope I can do this again next year.

Focusing on the Learner This Observation-level reflection is characteristic of a young child at the concrete-operational stage of development. This young student is relating to this service-learning experience on an individual rather than a societal level, which reflects her link to the concrete world. Issues of society involve more abstract levels of reasoning, which is difficult for students at this developmental stage to comprehend.

School Supplies for Kenya

"So the point of this class assignment is for you to practice citizenship," the high school social studies teacher announced. "How do we do that?" a student asked. "I've been in touch with a missionary from Kenya who works in a school there. They need books and supplies for the school. The school system has donated all the old textbooks they have on hand so we just need to collect money to buy supplies and then mail everything, which will be expensive," the teacher responded. So started this Community-Service service-learning experience.

"This is Tracy from Mr. Wray's social studies class," the student announced over the intercom. "We are sponsoring a school supplies drive for a school in Kenya. We have been given old textbooks by the county. Now we need to raise money to buy other school supplies and to pay for the mailing. We are taking up donations before school, during lunch, and at the basketball games. Please give what you can, and thanks in advance!"

Two months later, the class was working hard to box up the donated books and the supplies they had bought for the Kenyan school. After the last of the tape had been applied, the teacher settled the class down and started a class discussion by asking questions such as: How do you feel looking at all the boxes heading for Kenya? Do you think helping to raise money for the Kenya project was a good use of your time? Were you pleased with how the other students in school responded? Did working on this project impact your opinion of what being a good citizen means? How?

At first the students were a little timid in responding honestly to their teacher's questions, but then a lively discussion began. During the discussion, the students decided that they needed to write an intercom announcement thanking their schoolmates and the staff for all their donations and letting them know that the books and school supplies were boxed and ready to be shipped. As their final assignment, Mr. Wray asked the class to write a reflective essay connecting what they learned from the Kenya project to citizenship in their own community.

An example of a reflection follows:

> I came in early three days a week to bring the *Coins for Kenya* milk jug around to all the kids gathered in groups on the grass by our school's main entrance. I kinda enjoyed doing this because I got to see my

friends although it was tough getting to school early! I collected $16.75, which isn't much, but every little bit helps, as they say.

After we learned about how poor the people in Kenya were and what their everyday life was like, I began to realize that our old textbooks and some new school supplies might really help the students there. By the time we got to go to the store to buy the school supplies, I was really excited about the project and proud to be a part of it. It felt kinda good to help somebody. I hope the missionary in Kenya writes back and lets us know how the kids in his school liked what we sent.

We are supposed to connect this to being good citizens. I guess I learned that being a good citizen can be more than just following the rules or not breaking a law. Good citizens become involved and help others.

Focusing on the Learner What is the learner doing here? He is relating the situation. It's as if he is a correspondent reporting on the events—nothing more, nothing less. This example definitely slots into Observation-level reflection. At one point he mentions that it "felt kinda good to help somebody," but there was no elaboration about this. What does "kinda good" mean? How will this feeling affect him in the future? How has it altered his views on the people he is helping or his views on helping others in general? He came close to analysis when he stated, "I guess I learned that being a good citizen can be more than just following the rules or not breaking a law." As any teacher will tell you, however, this is more typical of a student who is responding to the requirements of the assignment, not a student who has really had an insight. The "I guess" is the first clue that this student is reaching for something to add.

Ask the Experts

1. *I work in the guidance office of a large urban high school. The students are required to perform 100 hours of service-learning in order to graduate. Part of my job is to track and validate their service hours. Most of the students have time for only Community-Service–level activities. Your typology seems to indicate that Community-Service service-learning is inappropriate for high school students. Is this true? What would you suggest?*

Generally speaking high school students should participate at a higher level of service-learning than Community-Service, one more appropriate to their cognitive level. It's hard to tell from your question if the required 100 hours you mentioned are simple volunteer hours or service-learning. If the students are providing service with no connection to the curriculum and no formal reflection, they aren't participating in service-learning, even at the Community-Service level. We recognize that high school students are often involved in extracurricular activities or after-school jobs, making it hard to find time for service-learning at any level. Your school has already made a commitment to having its students provide service in the community; here are a few suggestions to help you ensure that it is indeed service-learning. Working with your community partners, create a comprehensive list of service possibilities in your community. From this list and other content-related service ideas teachers may have, ask each teacher involved to create a class list of service possibilities related to his or her specific subject matter area(s). The students would then be required to choose a service option from the class list and, at a minimum, reflect upon how the service performed impacts their community and themselves. Both group and individual service experiences can be handled in this manner. If you want to encourage higher-level service-learning, you may want to employ a weighted system when tracking the service hours. For instance, each hour of Community-Exploration might be counted as one and a half hours with each hour of Community-Action doubled. In other words, fifteen hours of Community-Service would be worth fifteen service hours; fifteen hours of Community-Exploration might be worth twenty-two and a half service hours; and fifteen hours of Community-Action service-learning might be worth thirty of the required 100 service hours. Of course, encouraging higher-level service-learning in your school also requires a greater commitment from each teacher who agrees to facilitate service-learning in his or her classroom. Please see Chapters 3 and 4 for specifics on Community-Exploration and Community-Action service-learning.

2. *Why does volunteerism seem to have a negative connotation to service-learning advocates? Isn't helping your neighbors important in fostering good character?*

Simple volunteer activities, usually sponsored in the community by scouts, church youth groups, or other youth-serving organizations, can play a vital role in building positive self-esteem in children and contributing to the community. Getting positive feedback for his or her efforts usually encourages a young person to want to help others again, thus planting the seeds of good character development. Simple volunteerism, however, does not focus on the academic outcomes that service-learning promotes. Though recognizing the benefits of volunteerism such as promoting self-responsibility and improvement in school attendance, service-learning advocates encourage service-learning over volunteerism because of the connection to curriculum objectives.

References

Bloom, Benjamin S., ed. 1956. *Taxonomy of Educational Objectives: The Classification of Educational Goals: Handbook I, Cognitive Domain.* New York: Longmans, Green.

Bradley, James. 1995. "A Model for Evaluating Student Learning in Academically Based Service." In *Connecting Cognition and Action: Evaluation of Student Performance in Service Learning Courses,* edited by M. Troppe, 13–26. Providence, RI: Campus Compact.

Henderson, Bruce. 1987. "The Kids Who Saved a Dying Town." *Reader's Digest,* September, 42–46.

Piaget, Jean. 1950. *The Psychology of Intelligence.* San Diego: Harcourt Brace Jovanovich.

Webb, Norman. 1999. "Alignment of Science and Mathematics Standards and Assessments in Four States: Research Monograph No. 18."

Chapter Three

Community-Exploration
Service-Learning

Introduction

> The merchants were asked, "How would you rate the downtown
> area for quality of eating places, parking, cleanliness of streets?"
> "What do you think is the primary reason why people don't shop in
> Royston?" "What kinds of improvements would you like to see?"
> (Henderson 1987, 44)

The RIPPLES Gang set out to explore their community and gather information about the community challenges they determined to be
significant issues. They investigated old newspapers from the beginning of the twentieth century, during the early years of Royston,
where they learned about real issues faced by Royston's earliest citizens. They attended a state-sponsored program in a nearby town that
addressed community revitalization through historic preservation.
They met with a University of Georgia Historic Preservation class
where they learned about different periods of architecture and the
importance of preserving old buildings and houses. They met with
the Southern Business Development Center at the University of
Georgia where they learned about the importance of marketing strategies to enhance community development. Several consultants came
to speak to their class: a Department of Transportation official; a state
consultant on community development; a Main Street representative;
and a city council member. They took notes, Matt drew pictures, and
they asked a lot of questions. After exploring their community and

Figure 3–1

Interaction between the school and community can go in either direction—the students go out into the community or elements of the community come into the school.

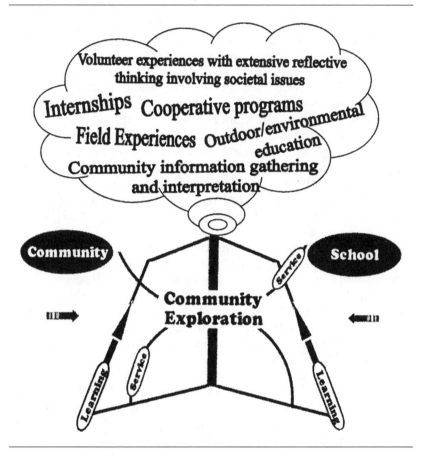

compiling what they had learned, the RIPPLES Gang had a more complete picture of the issues facing their town and how they might be addressed.

Community-Exploration service-learning entails not only awareness but exploration and engagement in the community as well. The students go out into the community or elements of the community come into the school where information from the real world is shared and explored at a more authentic level than the distancing abstraction of a textbook. Community-Exploration connects classroom learning to real-life situations. Schools can incorporate service-learning into the curriculum through a broad spectrum of classes including civics, art, science, history, health, language arts, reading, and computer technology. This practice involves tying the student service to an activity related to a specific area of study so the students can explore, research, and connect the selected classroom topic to a similar issue in the community. Community-Exploration service-learning is different from a standard independent study or research project in that it goes beyond just recalling and understanding basic facts about a community issue to defining and addressing an area of concern by applying the acquired knowledge in a resourceful manner.

Community-Exploration also includes activities that have usually been associated with experiential education but not always with service-learning, such as internships, outdoor/environmental education programs, and other types of experiential education. Community-Exploration does not necessarily involve direct service to the community although it may involve a high degree of learning as well as indirect service to the community.

For instance, student interns are usually placed at a site in the community that can utilize and broaden the student's academic or vocational skills. To be considered service-learning, the student must be placed with a service-oriented organization/business without being paid for the service provided, although reimbursement for expenses incurred is certainly allowable. The student also must make the necessary connections between the school curriculum and the internship experience through reflections on the academic content as well as on the service he or she provides. During this type of experience, a student intern learns firsthand about his or her field of interest and how to interact with the world of work, make decisions, and assume responsibility for his or her actions. Interning can enhance a student's personal, social, and academic growth and can involve him or her providing a great deal of direct service to the community through the work done during the internship, depending upon the nature of the internship experience. Indirect service is also provided to the community by giving students the experience of working in the real world, thus preparing them for a time when they will be fully contributing participants in the community.

Students engaged in Community-Exploration experiences gain academic learning and enabling skills; they also learn about their communities and how things operate in the real world. The greater the service and learning, the higher the degree on the service-learning typology thermometer (see chart in Appendix B).

Figure 3–2

The Best-Practice Model for Community-Exploration Service-Learning

The Best-Practice Model for Community-Exploration follows the standard service-learning steps of Preparation, Action, Reflection, and Celebration. During the Preparation step, the teacher should determine which piece of the curriculum might lend itself best to a service-learning approach. Consideration should also be given to identifying the type of Community-Exploration experience that is the most appropriate for the students involved, such as participating in a group experience, an individual experience, or an internship. The teacher should then facilitate a content-related discussion of the topic or subject matter and have the students brainstorm ideas concerning the topic that might be explored in their community.

The Action (Exploration) step of the Community-Exploration Best-Practice Model involves an authentic exploration of the community. During this step, the students go out into the community to research an area of interest and/or invite experts in the community to come into the classroom to share their knowledge. Students may also gain knowledge of the issue by interning with a community partner. The teacher should monitor the students' research or internships as well as oversee how they apply and analyze what they have learned. The students should connect their new community-based knowledge to the classroom topic and apply it in a meaningful manner by creating a useful product, ideally to be shared with others.

Reflection is the next step in the Community-Exploration Best-Practice Model. If the service-learning activity involves individual issues with the students operating at the lower level of Community-Exploration, the teacher should guide the students in their reflections to examine the experience at the Observation level. If the activity involves societal issues and the students are operating at the higher level of Community-Exploration, the teacher can guide them to assess the service experience at the Analysis level of reflection.

Celebration is the final and overarching component of this model. During this step, the student work should be acknowledged and validated as appropriate to the accomplishments of the Community-Exploration experience.

Logistics of Community-Exploration Service-Learning

In Community-Exploration service-learning, the actual service-learning experience can take place either inside the school, especially when community experts come into the classroom to share their knowledge, or outside of school, when the students leave the classroom to investigate and explore the situation in the community. In either case, good communication and coordination between the school and the community are a must. After the students have brainstormed content-related ideas that might be explored in the community, the teacher must contact the community partner(s) or site(s) to be visited as well as gain approval for the field trip from school administrators and parents. As with any school experience that takes place outside of school, the teacher must consider transportation needs and liability issues. Much of this planning depends on specific school district regulations; the teacher should become knowledgeable about the requirements of his or her school and system situation during the preparation stage.

Using parents as chaperones or to provide transportation is an alternative that usually encourages a broader understanding of the experience from the parents involved as well as more enthusiastic support for the service-learning experience.

Facilitating internships involves additional logistical concerns both before and during the placement. If the community is not familiar with service-learning internships, the teacher may need to educate local leaders, organizations, and businesses on what service-learning is and how it might be helpful to their organization and the community in general. The manual, *Partner Power and Service-Learning,* from ServeMinnesota is a very helpful resource in developing partnerships. It can be downloaded at www.serveminnesota.org /resources_serviceLearning_manual.php. After interest is established, the teacher must determine the expectations of the businesses or community-based organizations (CBO) as well as the expectations and goals of the school and the roles and responsibility of each partner (intern, school, and CBO/business) so that the students and their placements are well matched. It is also important to set up a detailed schedule as to when the students will be working in the community and determine who their supervisors will be. Other considerations might include sign-in procedures, on-the-job safety issues, background checks of staff and students, and tracking the students' time and effort.

Community-Exploration and Cognitive Development

Community-Exploration corresponds with either stage three or four of Piaget's cognitive development stages. If the activity involves individual issues and Observation-level reflection, it is classified as Piaget's stage three, the Concrete Operational stage. If the activity involves societal issues and Analysis-level reflection, it is classified as stage four, the Formal Operational stage (see the Developmental Service-Learning Typology chart in Appendix B). At this stage, students are capable of relating to the abstract issues and concerns of society.

Community-Exploration and Critical Thinking

Community-Exploration connects to Bloom's first three or four levels of the taxonomy (Bloom 1956): Knowledge, Comprehension, Application, and—when students are operating at a higher degree of Community-Exploration—Analysis. It relates to the first two or three levels of Webb's Depth of Knowledge (Webb 1999): recall, basic application of skill and content, and strategic thinking at the higher degree of Community-Exploration. In addition to recalling and understanding facts and basic concepts, students solve problems by applying acquired knowledge in a different way. At the highest degree of Community-Exploration, they examine and break apart information, make inferences, and find evidence to support generalizations. Participating in their service-learning experience, students at the higher level (see page 26 for lower level Community-Exploration questions) might attempt to answer questions such as:

- What examples can you find to illustrate your finding?
- What questions would you ask in an interview?
- How would you organize the information acquired to show your understanding of the community need or the service you provided as an intern?
- How would you categorize this information? How would you classify it?
- What inferences can you make? What conclusions can you draw?
- What would you do differently? How would these changes impact the service recipient?
- What is the relationship between this situation and others that are similar or quite different?
- What learning occurred that can be applied to other areas?
- What connections can you make between the service you provided as an intern and the curriculum in your school class?

Reflection During Community-Exploration

In Community-Exploration service-learning, the type of reflection carried out by the students at the higher developmental level is termed *Analysis*. At this level, reflections may be fairly thorough and accurate, and there may be hints to broader links, but, generally, students do not mention the bigger system in which the element is rooted. Students are, however, beginning to demonstrate an ability to read between the lines and explain the significance of what they have experienced (Bradley 1995). For those students operating at the lower developmental level of Community-Exploration, please see "Reflection During Community-Service" in Chapter 2 for an explanation of the Observation level of reflection and related Observation-level reflective activities. At the Analysis level, youth:

- Provide reflections that are fairly comprehensive with some awareness of the subtle shades of meaning without necessarily considering the broader situation.

- Relate a convincing account from one perspective although not necessarily connecting it beyond the immediate experience/situation or to factors that illustrate how difficult change is to accomplish.

- Present both *personal beliefs* as well as *evidence* and show a beginning ability to explain the difference between the two.

- Identify and understand justifiable differences of perspective.

- Display an emerging capacity to understand and interpret evidence.

Suggestions for Reflective Activities at the Analysis Level of Community-Exploration

- Students can write a thorough weekly summary of the Community-Exploration (CE) experience describing their observations and sharing any personal beliefs as well as evidence from the experience.

- Students can discuss their experiences extensively during a class discussion period, relating their observations and opinions. Students should have an opportunity to recognize legitimate differences of view that may exist among class members and others.

- Students can debate issues relating to the CE experience. This does not need to relate to a broader context of the situation, just to the situation in which they are involved.

- Students can express their feelings about their CE experience through the use of poetry, drawing, cartooning, painting, music, or dance. They can perform this task from a specific point of view about the CE experience.

- Students can write letters of inquiry about something involving their CE activity. They can express points of view and interpret any evidence they have.

- Students can create a scrapbook and/or portfolio that document all the evidence of their activities.

- Students can create a detailed timeline of the service-learning experience.

- Students can design a webpage that relates activities and experiences of the CE activities. These activities can reflect personal beliefs and differing points of view as well as evidence the students have acquired about their CE activity.

- Students can design a bulletin board dealing with different viewpoints concerning their CE activities. Including sections titled "Pros" and "Cons" can be effective.

Starter Ideas for Community-Exploration Activities

As in Community-Service, the following ideas are intended to be a springboard for helping to connect service-learning to both your curriculum and a concern in your community. After each activity, symbols have been added to denote a specific curriculum area connection (CC). LA represents language/arts; M represents math; SC represents science; SS represents social studies; A represents art; and CT represents computer technology. Adaptations will probably need to be made to these starter ideas depending upon the content area you teach. Please note: suggestions in *italic* denote a Community-Exploration service idea that can be elevated to a Community-Action experience with more commitment to and impact on the need area; a deeper interaction between the service provider and service recipient; and a higher level of reflection.

- Contact the high school band teacher and others involved in art and music to investigate interest in organizing a community chorus, band, or art league. Help publicize the tryouts (CC: M, SS, A).
- Create a brochure and/or map listing the special attractions or historical places in your community. Give the map to a civic club to duplicate and distribute it to businesses, households, schools, and community centers (CC: SS, A, CT).
- *Petition the city council to renovate an abandoned building or house. Research possible civic uses for the property, such as a home for abused women and their children, an after-school facility, a senior citizen center, or a hands-on museum. Present your ideas to the mayor and city council* (CC: LA, SS).
- Intern at a public radio or TV station (CC: LA, SS).
- *Research the town history; create pictures that represent the history. Suggest that the art class paint wall murals based on the town history drawings or give the drawings to community artists to paint the murals* (CC: SS, A).
- Intern at a local art museum (CC: SS, A).
- *Survey residents on neighborhood crime; interview police and town officials on prevention methods. Compile the results and give them to the police department and/or city council* (CC: LA, M if charts and graphs are used, SS).

- *Interview senior citizens, veterans, and older residents about the town's history. Create a bulletin board in the school about the history of the community* (CC: LA, SS).
- Intern at a local history museum (CC: SS).
- *Research the pre-reading skills needed to become a reader. Create action games for young children to encourage those skills, and give them to a pre-school teacher to use with his or her students* (CC: LA, SS).
- Intern at the town library or records center (CC: LA, SS).
- Interview and highlight new students for the school paper in order to help new students feel welcome (CC: LA, SS).
- *Learn about water-quality testing. Test the local streams, rivers, lakes, and water-storage facilities for the presence of pollutants. Compile the findings and give to the local agency that oversees water-quality control* (CC: SC, M if charts and graphs are used).
- Intern at a zoological garden, nature habitat, or environmental center (CC: SC).
- Intern with the Parks Department or Forestry Service (CC: SC).
- Research the trees and plants that grow best in your area. Study birds and small animals native to your area. Write an informative article for your school or community newspaper (CC: LA, SC).
- *Survey the school to determine the use and disposal of environmentally unfriendly materials. Investigate safer alternatives and present your findings to the principal, school board, or PTA* (CC: if charts and graphs are used, SC).
- *Investigate recycling efforts in your community. Present your results to the city council* (CC: SC).
- *Study the impact of poor air quality on plants, animals, and humans. Conduct various air quality samplings throughout your community. Report your findings in the school or community newspaper* (CC: SC).
- Survey the students in your grade or school to find out if they smoke cigarettes and relate the results on a bulletin board in the school using graphs and charts (CC: M, SS).
- Arrange for experts to present at an assembly in your school on the dangers of smoking and survey the impact of the assembly on the students and staff (CC: SC, SS).
- Intern at your local or county health center (CC: SC).
- Intern at the Red Cross, Cancer Society, Kidney Foundation, or health department (CC: SC, SS).
- *Collect and document what life was like during recent historical periods by interviewing residents of nursing homes, veterans' hospitals, and*

rehabilitation centers. Create an oral history page for the town or school website (CC: LA, SS, CT).

- Design flyers or webpages for local nonprofits so that more people are aware of their services (CC: SS, A, CT).

- Design personalized software for local nonprofits to better track volunteers, community needs. and/or donations (CC: SS, CT).

- Intern at the local Department of Human Services (CC: SS).

- *Survey grocery stores and local restaurants to find out what they do with their outdated and unused food. Compile the results and give them to homeless shelters and similar organizations* (CC: SS).

Examples of Community-Exploration Service-Learning

Student Bicentennial Project

Mr. Latham stood before his eighth-grade state history class and asked if the students wanted to help out with the bicentennial celebrations planned for early spring. He was on the community's Bicentennial Committee and had tentatively offered the services of his classes to help with projects that were being considered. With the exception of one of his classes, all responded with restrained enthusiasm. The promise of free cotton candy during the celebration week turned that restraint into complete enthusiasm!

Thus began the *Student Bicentennial Project*. Recognizing that he needed to focus first and foremost on his course objectives, Mr. Latham pulled objectives from both the social studies curriculum and the character education curriculum mandated by the state. The Woman's Club was creating a quilt for the celebration that would be hung in the courthouse as a permanent reminder of both the celebration and the community's history. The quilt was going to focus on the historical properties of the community. Accompanying the quilt would be a detailed reference book and a CD that would document the history and description of each property that was represented on each block on the quilt. Mr. Latham knew this project would help him teach the history of the community—objectives he had to teach.

The Bicentennial Committee gave Mr. Latham a list of the properties that would be included in the project. Mr. Latham assigned each property to teams of three students. The students were to research their property and write up their findings in a report, which would be combined and given to the Bicentennial Committee to make into a book and a CD. Two field trips were planned: one to the courthouse to investigate the history of each property, and one to visit the properties on the quilt and take digital photographs. The courthouse trip was limited to the group-elected researcher in each group since taking almost a hundred students to the courthouse would be unwieldy. The trip to take the digital photographs included all students involved in the project, although the actual photos were taken by the group-elected photographer in each group.

Over the course of four months, the students spent most Fridays working on the project. Mr. Latham compacted the curriculum somewhat for the four classes involved in the project. They followed the county curriculum map, which was something each eighth-grade teacher had to follow sequentially. However, Mr. Latham covered the week's county curriculum objectives Monday through Thursday, if at all possible, through curriculum compacting. This meant that students had more homework during the week, but they didn't seem to mind because they enjoyed working on the Bicentennial Project. They were self-directed and involved with their research. They conducted interviews with people about their property; they examined legal documents recorded at the courthouse; they examined all evidence collected; they researched architectural designs; and each group documented its work weekly.

The students were honored during Bicentennial Week in the spring at the community barbeque. The Bicentennial Committee took the research reports completed by the students and put them into a book that a local publisher published. A CD was also created from the electronic submissions the students had done. The Bicentennial Committee made both pieces available for sale, with proceeds going to the local historical society.

This Community-Exploration service-learning experience qualifies as a high-level experience because of the high level of reflection Mr. Latham incorporated. Once a month during the service-learning experience, he assembled the class and had them share their research to date. To evoke a higher level of critical thinking, he asked them questions, such as the following:

- How does the style of this property compare to the style of this other one? Why are they different?

- Does the architectural style reflect what was going on in the development of the community at that time? How?

- What inferences can you make about the lives of the people who lived during the time this building was erected? How does that differ from this other property that was built much later?

- How might we compare the builders of this building to the builders of the new bank in town?
- Is it important to document these properties? Why? What difference might this documentation make down the road?
- How do you feel about documenting this history for the future?
- Might this documentation ensure that these building aren't torn down in the future? Is that important? Why?

At the end of the experience, as their summative assessment each group presented their project to the class, including the photographs they took. In addition to relating the information about their research, the students were required to answer the following questions:

- What have you learned about involvement in a community? How did you feel working on this project for the community?
- What would you do differently in this project if you began again? Would these changes impact the community? How?

An example of a summative reflection at the Community-Exploration Analysis level to answer the previously listed questions follows:

Getting involved with the community was a lot more fun and rewarding than we ever expected. Mrs. Knowles could be a little irritating at times (like when she pinched our cheeks!), but pretty much everybody was really nice to us and appreciated what we did. I mean, it wasn't that big of a deal, but you would've thought we were war heroes the way they went on and on about how great we were at the barbeque. I don't know what we'll do with a key to the city, but it was a cool thing to get (too bad it won't unlock the bank's safe! Just kidding!). Most of the things we do in school are just for a grade. This was bigger than that and we didn't do it for the grade—at least not after we started it. We did it because it was interesting and because we felt it was important. The stuff we found out was really cool, and because we did it, people in a hundred years will know more about our community. That's neat. The good grade was nice, but it's not why we did it. We did it because we thought it was important and we wanted to do a good job for our city and for us. It sounds stupid, but one day we could take our grandchildren down to the courthouse to see the quilt and the book that was made because of our research. I think if we had to start over again, we would have contacted more people who knew about the history of the hardware store—people who had owned it and might have had pictures and stuff. Henry's group did that and they got some great pictures to add to their report. I think we might like to find out more about old documents, too. Some of the stuff didn't make a lot of sense. It would have been nice if we had gotten somebody who knows about that stuff to sit down with us and make some sense of parts of it. We don't know if we could have done any more on the project to make it better—maybe getting more old pictures might have. But it was a great project, so I don't think we would change much. It's the best thing we've done in school all year. We just hate that it's over now.

Focusing on the Learner The preceding reflection is written at the Analysis level, which means the writer was performing at the highest level of Community-Exploration service-learning. The writer has gone beyond just relating what was done during the project, as in Observation-level reflection, and is analyzing what was learned from doing this Community-Exploration experience—what it meant personally. However, the reflection isn't going beyond the activity in which the writer was involved, as one would do at the Synthesis level of reflection.

Student Service-Learning Advisory Board

Ms. Frederick, civics teacher for the high school, was called in by the principal to discuss some ideas the principal had for her civics class. These ideas soon became the impetus for a Community-Exploration service-learning experience that led to the establishment of the Student Service-Learning Advisory Board for the school. The school had adopted service-learning as part of its mission statement during the previous school year. The principal decided to establish a student advisory board that would look into service opportunities in the school and the community and work with the Community-Faculty Advisory Board, which had the goal of implementing and sustaining the spirit of service in the school.

Ms. Frederick asked her fifth-period civics class if they would like to become the Student Advisory Board. She reminded them of some of the lessons they learned in civics class and how this activity would fit into the curriculum objectives. Most of the class agreed, but the students didn't know where to start or even if organizations would accept volunteers less than eighteen years of age. One of the boys thought that volunteering sounded too much like the community service work that you had to do when you got in trouble. Another said that he didn't have time to volunteer with homework, chores, band practice, and his part-time job to worry about. The class voted, deciding that it could research volunteer opportunities in the school and town and then let the Community-Faculty Advisory Board know about them.

Using the telephone book and the town website, the students put together a list of all the community agencies that served people living in Clinton. Ms. Frederick assigned each student one or two agencies to research the agencies' main focus, how people applied for their services, how many people they served, and if they would be open to using student volunteers. Two students looked into the legal issues of students under eighteen years old doing service in the community. They even invited a local attorney come to their class to discuss the legal issues with them. The class found this presentation interesting.

Because Ms. Frederick compacted the civics curriculum, the class was usually able to spend one class period a week on this project. After the students reported on what they found out about their assigned agencies, they realized that they had left out some important groups that might need assistance, such as the recreational sports leagues, the parks department, and nursing homes. They went back to work, creating a more comprehensive list of organizations to survey. Because their list of potential service recipients was now so long, they emailed the survey to all the organizations, associations, civic groups, churches, and businesses listed on the town's website.

The students' next task was to make the other students and faculty in their school aware of what they were doing. They wrote up a variety of announcements and got approval to read a forty-five-second message every Wednesday during the morning announcements. After compiling all the surveys, the class decided that it needed to post the volunteer opportunities on the school's website. They got Ms. Walker, the school's technology teacher, involved in helping them, and she designed a webpage that linked to both the school and town websites.

When Ms. Frederick asked the class to reflect on what they had accomplished and what it meant to the community, the class members realized how important the project had become to them. The class members felt good about what they had started and felt confident that the Student Advisory Board would continue for many years to come.

An example of a summative reflection at the Community-Exploration Analysis level follows:

> When Ms. Frederick asked us to think about all that we had accomplished, I realized how much my opinion of doing service work had changed. I had kinda [sic] thought of it only as a way to work out a punishment when you got caught, like my neighbor Tommy had to do. This was different. We learned a lot about Clinton, and I think Clinton learned a lot about us. We also learned about legal issues when the lawyer came and talked to us. I hadn't thought of that before and thought it was really interesting. It made me think that I might want to be a lawyer one day.
>
> I think our project was very successful, and now I really get what it means to be a good citizen, to practice citizenship. Although we didn't walk old people across a busy street, we did research stuff about groups in our community that might need some help. Then we gave that information to the Community-Faculty Advisory Board so

that they could use our information to help lots of people in Clinton and that was neat. We also learned how to write and send out surveys and how to track them, too. Service-learning is not like doing homework where we just put it in a folder and throw it away later. I'm kinda [sic] proud that I helped to put together something that will help our school and town for now and in the future.

Focusing on the Learner The preceding reflection was written at the Analysis level. It does have some Observation-level reflection in relating what was learned, but the writer has analyzed the experience rather well. The writer analyzed his changed viewpoint of service-learning and noted his new feelings about it, relating how proud he was to have helped put together something that would help his community now and in the future. While Community-Exploration comprises two levels, one of which relates to individual issues and Observation-level reflection, and the higher level relating to societal issues and Analysis-level reflection, we would expect a high-school student working on a project with societal impact to be functioning at the Analysis-level of reflection. In reality, this is not always the case. Reflection utilizes creative- and critical-thinking processes to help youth convert their service experience into a productive learning experience. For some students this may be the first time in their school career that they have been asked to analyze a situation. It is easier to slip back into the more familiar Observation-level of thinking and reflecting. The beauty of service-learning is that it fosters growth to the next higher level. Teachers should be aware that mixed reflection levels may occur at first within the same submission. They also may find that different students working on the same project could function at conjoining levels of reflection. That is why it is so important to focus on the learner, always encouraging him or her to achieve higher levels of thinking and reflecting.

Ask the Experts

1. *Some of the most stunning service-learning projects I have seen involved original social or environmental research done by students that was then submitted to city officials. It seems more to be Community-Exploration since the students didn't take action on their findings, though the learning couldn't have been greater. Could you tell me where this work would fit into the typology?*

This would most definitely fit into Community-Exploration service-learning. In Community-Exploration service-learning, there is usually a great deal of learning as the students explore their community. The greater the learning, the higher the degree on the service-learning thermometer. There can also be a good deal of service when students do original social and environmental research and give it to officials to take action on it. A good example is a group of students one of the authors worked with that researched waste disposal options in their county and reported their findings to the county commissioners. Along the way, they debunked one proposal as an option for the five-county regional group to consider due to the waste stream analysis they had done. But you are right. It is not Community-Action service-learning because the students themselves did not take action on it, at least not at that point. I must disagree with your comment that "the learning couldn't have been greater." Indeed the learning is greater in Community-Action service-learning because, in addition to doing the exploration in the Community-Exploration phase of the experience, the students are using high-level skills in solving the problem themselves, not handing over that responsibility to someone else. That neither minimizes nor marginalizes the efforts of students who perform at the Community-Exploration level at all! When you focus on the learner, however, there is a greater degree of learning for the student in the highest—Community-Action—level of service-learning. Students are doing advanced problem solving and taking action accordingly based on the exploration they have already done. A teacher must examine his or her curriculum objectives first and foremost and base the service-learning experience on those needs.

2. *Seeing that there is not always a lot of direct service in Community-Exploration, please explain how service-learning at this level is different from an independent study project?*

This depends on how you define service. If a student does an independent study on a Civil War battlefield in his or her community by reading existing books on it and doing a report, it is not service-learning. If the student does firsthand research, investigating primary sources that lead to new information or a new interpretation of history and the student shares this newfound knowledge, then a service to the community is involved and service-learning has indeed taken place. There is a second argument for this being service-learning even if the student doesn't share the knowledge. If he or she is somehow changed by the experience, such as having it affect his or her life choices, that is indirect service. Indirect service is not something we can see the effects of immediately, but it is of service in the future when that student perhaps becomes a historian or a teacher as result of the experience. Admittedly this is a gray area and ultimately is up to the school whether to term such activities as service-learning.

3. *It seems to me that you have to go to a huge amount of effort to set up effective internships. What's the best way to begin? How are service-learning internships different from school-to-work programs?*

Setting up effective internships certainly is challenging. There is an excellent resource available online as a downloadable PDF file, *Partner Power and Service-Learning,* which can be helpful in starting an internship program in your school and community (see www.serveminnesota.org /resources_serviceLearning_manual.php). School-to-work programs generally involve more private-sector partnerships with the learning being personal to the student, while service-learning usually involves personal learning with a public benefit. School-to-work programs can be service-learning, depending on several things. First, the placement must be with organizations involved in public service such as Family and Children Services, animal shelters, the Main Street program, or even the service arm of a business. Second, there must be appropriate reflective activities set up and maintained throughout the internship. Finally, the students should not be paid for their work, although they can be reimbursed for expenses incurred. The program should be set up carefully, matching service opportunities with students' interests. Reflective activities should be addressed formally before students begin their service activities. Weekly journal reflections centered on questions appropriate for the Community-Exploration level of service-learning are effective at promoting learning for the students. Students need to reflect not only on the content-specific learning but on the service-specific learning as well.

4. *I have third-grade students who visited nursing home residents on a regular basis and wrote a biography of them, with one copy going to the senior citizen and one to the school library. According to your typology, this project seems to be in the middle ground of Community-Exploration and Community-Action, but seemed more in Community-Exploration, despite the value. Where would this project fit and why?*

This type of service-learning experience is very beneficial to the community, the students, and senior citizens. There is both service and learning in this project. Assuming there is a link to the curriculum and, at the least, Observation-level reflective activities, this would fall into Community-Exploration due the high degree of learning embedded in the program. If the students had not written the biography of the seniors and had just visited the nursing home and done Observation-level reflections, this would have been a Community-Service service-learning experience.

5. *As a follow-up to the previous question, I have seen this particular model— biographies of senior citizens written by students from a local school—in a* *number of different sites, with a range from first-grade to high-school authors. Some of the projects and partnerships were incredible in quality and depth; some were not well done at all. Isn't this more an issue not of what "developmental stage" they represented but what attributes of planning and project design make for important and effective learning experiences. How do you respond to that?*

Program design is very important, especially in service-learning. In general, poorly designed service-learning programs create poorly executed programs regardless of the developmental level of the students. Using this typology, a teacher may think he or she has set up a Community-Action experience, but if it the program design is poorly implemented, it will certainly fall short of this high level of service-learning. Poor implementation can take many forms. If the students are not given opportunities for appropriate reflective activities, then learning, particularly concerning the service aspect, may not be what it should be. In conducting research, one of the authors investigated a service-learning experience that was outstanding except for the opportunities for reflection. As a result, the students interviewed had serious misalignments of factual events and what they meant, to the point that one group had developed a presentation but the students didn't know who it was for or why they were doing it. If the teacher had allowed even informal reflection through discussion, she would have realized how confused the students were about what they were doing. She was an excellent teacher, but as she articulated, "There just wasn't time for reflection."

Sometimes well-meaning teachers *conduct* outstanding service-learning experiences with incredible results for the community. The problem is, because the teacher is *conducting* the experience, the students have neither *choice* nor *voice*. The community outcome may look awesome, but where is the learning for the students? That is why the typology is set up as it is: to focus the teacher's attention on the learner. If the teacher in the previous example had conducted appropriate synthesis-level reflective activities, she would have realized how confused the students were and could have helped the students clarify issues so the meaning would be clear.

References

Bloom, Benjamin S., ed. 1956. *Taxonomy of Educational Objectives: The Classification of Educational Goals: Handbook I, Cognitive Domain.* New York: Longmans, Green.

Bradley, James. 1995. "A Model for Evaluating Student Learning in Academically Based Service." In *Connecting Cognition and Action: Evaluation of Stu-*

dent Performance in Service Learning Courses, edited by M. Troppe, 13–26. Providence, RI: Campus Compact.

Henderson, Bruce. 1987. "The Kids Who Saved a Dying Town." *Reader's Digest,* September, 42–46.

Webb, Norman. 1999. "Alignment of Science and Mathematics Standards and Assessments in Four States: Research Monograph No. 18."

Chapter Four

Community-Action
Service-Learning

Now, sliding a chair over to the low table where the students were sitting, she [the teacher] asked a question. "Okay, we've identified some of our town's problems. What can we do to save Royston?" (Henderson 1987, 43)

Introduction

What indeed? Where to begin? The RIPPLES Gang had been exploring their community. After many weeks of in-depth exploration of the history of their town, historic preservation, market studies, and railroad policies, the students were ready to save their dying town. They began by reviewing their early list of identified challenges and added to that list what they had learned from the exploration of their community. Then they brainstormed a new list, a list of possible solutions to the challenges they had identified. There were too many to actually attempt them all, but they began to classify the list and then rank the items according to the importance of each. And then—and then they dug in. They designed a tentative plan of action and began implementing that action step by step, challenge by challenge.

Community-Action (CA) service-learning, the highest level on the service-learning continuum, involves youth not only becoming aware of, exploring, and becoming engaged in their community but also making a positive impact on their community and becoming empowered to make a difference in the real world (see the Developmental Service-Learning Typology chart in Appendix B) like the RIPPLES Gang was able to do (see Chapter 1).

Figure 4–1
Interaction between the school and community flows in
both directions, producing greater impact in the community
and empowerment in the students.

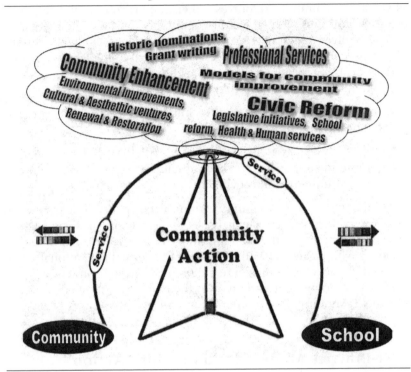

Community-Action results in students becoming aware of a need in the community and providing a service, but it can also lead to students becoming so engrossed in and committed to the need area that they go beyond just supplying a service. Students analyze the situation, generate new ideas, and implement a difference-making plan of action. In the process, the students develop complex problem-solving skills, advanced communication skills, the ability to connect knowledge across the disciplines, and the perseverance to overcome obstacles.

In Community-Action service-learning, the interaction between the students and community flows back and forth in both directions. This interaction leads to a broader community impact and the highest level of real-world learning. It also fosters reciprocity between the students and community, with both becoming learners and recipients of the service experience. Involvement in Community-Action service-learning often empowers students. They believe in their ability to make a difference, thereby becoming more responsive, effective citizens. The community, in turn, develops a respect and appreciation for the positive change brought about by the students and begins to perceive its youth as valuable community resources rather than as community responsibilities or problems with which the community must deal. Community-Action involves a high degree of service, producing a broader community impact and the highest degree of learning (see the Developmental Service-Learning Typology chart in Appendix B).

Activities in Community-Action service-learning can include:

- Civic reform, such as legislative initiatives, school improvement, and health and human service ventures
- Professional services, such as historic nominations and grant writing
- Community enhancement, such as cultural and aesthetic ventures and environmental improvement

Students at the Community-Action level of service-learning are involved with abstract societal issues and concerns and the highest level of reflection, Synthesis. Community-Action service-learning corresponds with Piaget's (1950) stage four, the Formal Operational stage, of cognitive development where children can form abstractions from concrete experiences. It also involves the highest levels of cognition in Bloom's Taxonomy, Synthesis and Evaluation.

Best-Practice Model for Community-Action Service-Learning

This three-dimensional graphic portrayal of the Community-Action best-practice model (see Figure 4–2) illustrates the depth and richness of the Community-Action experience. This service-learning model involves important and complex processes that lead to higher levels of learning for youth and greater service to the community. In Community-Action service-learning, the *preparation, action, reflection,* and *celebration* components are interwoven throughout the experience.

The Cognitive Apprenticeship Model

The cognitive apprenticeship model (Brown, Collins, and Duguid 1989) describes four elements that lead to learning: *scaffolding, modeling, coaching,* and *fading* (see page 82). The teacher or leader acts as a facilitator providing scaffolding until the students are ready to take on more re-

Figure 4–2

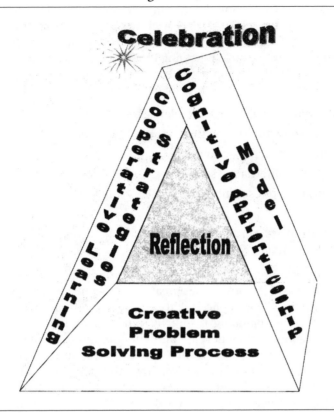

sponsibility for their learning. This model can be described as a hand-holding method that leads youth from dependence to independence in learning. It is important because it guides the students in becoming self-learners as they construct their own learning experiences by working cooperatively in their selected groups.

Although the teacher acts as facilitator in the classroom using this model, the classes are student-run, student-focused, and student-led. The cognitive apprenticeship model empowers the students within the classroom, thereby assuring more commitment to the project and more positive attitudes toward the experience.

The Creative Problem Solving Process

The creative problem solving process provides service-learning partici-pants with logical steps to follow from their initial investigation of community needs to the implementation of their difference-making plan of action. The Osborn-Parnes model of creative problem solving (Osborn 1963, Parnes 1967) has been a successful model for use in classrooms. E. Paul Torrance introduced this model into classrooms through the Future Problem Solving Program he and his wife, J. Pansy Torrance, initiated in the mid-1970s. The Osborn-Parnes creative problem solving process includes the following steps:

- Identifying problems and challenges.
- Recognizing and stating the important problem.
- Producing alternative solutions.
- Evaluating alternative solutions.
- Planning to put solutions into use. (Torrance 1995)

Creative Problem Solving Model for Community-Action Service-Learning

The model for Community-Action service-learning shown in Figure 4–3 follows the basic Osborn-Parnes creative problem solving process but relates it specifically to service-learning. The Community-Action model goes beyond just planning to put hypothetical solutions into use to guiding students as they develop authentic solutions, create an action plan, and actually implement their solution ideas in the community. The triangle in this model illustrates the basic steps in a Community-Action service-learning project. Each step builds upon the other, narrowing the focus until the apex of the triangle is reached—taking the Action.

The butterfly represents the direction the Community-Action service-learning experience may take. Following the wings takes students through different parts of the process interchangeably—flowing back and forth between the stages as needed during a Community-Action service-learning experience—in a circular, rather than linear direction. This process represents new challenges, new opportunities, and new directions. The butterfly also symbolizes the emergence of new life and an openness to change—freedom to grow. Taking action in their community leads students from the pupa stage of development to the butterfly stage of development—soaring to new heights!

This model is effective because it allows the students a *choice* and a *voice* in the service-learning activities, thereby helping to ensure more interest in the project. In other words, the students, not the teacher, are the ones who decide on the focus for the project. The teacher's role is to guide the students through the steps of the creative problem solving process. Using this process, the students identify challenges within

Figure 4–3

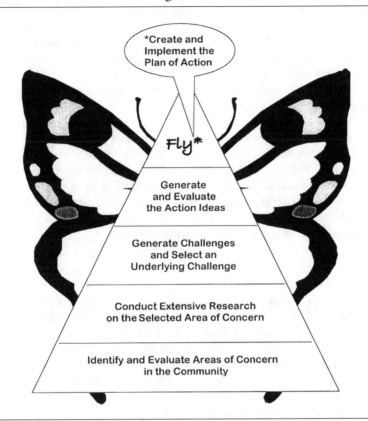

*Create and Implement the Plan of Action

Fly*

Generate and Evaluate the Action Ideas

Generate Challenges and Select an Underlying Challenge

Conduct Extensive Research on the Selected Area of Concern

Identify and Evaluate Areas of Concern in the Community

their own community and decide themselves which challenges they will address and what actions they will take while applying key curricular principles to overcome community challenges and extend their learning. The more *choice* and *voice* the students are given, the more interested and involved they will become both in the experience and in their community. This process not only makes the students feel their input is meaningful and valued but also encourages the development of leadership and organizational skills as well as personal responsibility.

Cooperative Learning

Cooperative learning strategies are key to successful youth-run service-learning. The learning takes place between youth participants through interaction with one another as they work in self-selected action groups (see Chapter 5) to carry out the piece of the action plan for which their group is responsible. The actual action groups will differ depending upon the focus of the project and the related curriculum objectives. The students in each group may work on different tasks at different paces within the group, but they all share the responsibility for implementation, record keeping, and assessment.

Research has shown that students working in cooperative learning groups not only enjoy the content better but also learn more about it than they do with traditional instruction from a teacher. In addition, it has been found that team members in cooperative group-learning settings gain self-esteem from their successes, and minority groups are more accepted by their peers as are handicapped students (Slavin 1986). When asked what he learned from participating in his Community-Action service-learning experience, one seventh-grade student responded that he had learned a lot of cooperation skills. A classmate added that he had learned a lot about teamwork.

Reflection

Reflection is the framework around which the students process and synthesize information and ideas they have gleaned during their service-learning activities (Alliance for Service Learning in Education Reform 1993). Reflection utilizes creative and critical thinking processes to help youth convert their service experience into a productive learning experience. Reflective activities are central to effective service-learning. It is important that teachers take the time to provide reflective activities that guide the students in developing a deeper and richer understanding of their service experience.

In Community-Action service-learning, the type of reflection carried out by the students is termed *Synthesis*. Students operating at this level see things from many perspectives and can make appropriate judgments based on reasoning and evidence (Bradley 1995). At this level, youth:

- Look at things from a variety of viewpoints and are able to put into context perceived differences within the situation.
- Are capable of appreciating conflicting ideas within the situation and of understanding that these ideas can be assessed.
- Understand that actions vary by situation and are able to recognize the many issues that affect their decision making.
- Formulate conclusions based on critical thinking and evidence.
- Evaluate the importance of the decisions facing the individuals and/ or community involved and of their responsibility as a part of it all.

Appropriate Reflective Activities for Community-Action Service-Learning

Students can perform the following reflective activities in Community-Action service-learning:

- Write a weekly reflection of the Community-Action (CA) experience describing, analyzing, and then putting their observations into a larger context. The students should relate any conflicting goals within the situation and assess the importance of any decisions facing those involved.

- Discuss their experiences extensively during a class discussion period relating their observations, opinions, and judgments. Students should have an opportunity to recognize legitimate differences of viewpoint that may exist among class members and others.

- Debate issues regarding the CA experience. This should relate to a broader context of the situation as well as to the situation itself.

- Express their feelings about their CA experience. They could do this through the use poetry, drawing, cartooning, painting, music, or dance. Encourage them to do this from a more universal point of view, connecting their CA experience to a broader context.

- Write letters, emails, or articles expressing opinions about something involving their CA service-learning experience.

- Create an annotated timeline of the service-learning experience.

- Create a scrapbook and/or portfolio that documents all the evidence of their activities, reflecting all aspects of the CA service-learning experience.

- Design a webpage relating their activities and experiences. These activities can reflect personal beliefs and differing points of view as well as evidence and judgments the students have formulated about their CA service-learning experience.

Celebration

Celebration is the use of multiple methods to acknowledge, celebrate, and further validate students' service work (Toole 1998). According to the National Service-Learning Cooperative, celebration is a critical component of service-learning that supports both learning and service. Celebration refers to opportunities that recognize and honor the good work students have done in making a positive difference in their community. Celebration is an overarching component of all levels of service-learning, and even more so for Community-Action service-learning. Higher levels of celebration can be paramount in helping students reach their developmental potential. Appendix B lists agencies, businesses, and competitions that can provide opportunities for celebration and demonstration, acknowledging the significant contributions that youth have made to the community. This recognition can range from awarding certificates and trophies to giving cash prizes or scholarships for individual or group efforts to providing an opportunity for students to display and demonstrate their work before a national or international audience.

Logistics of Community-Action Service-Learning

The logistics of a Community-Action project cannot be easily outlined, as the action in the community depends on the focus of the service-learning experience. Most Community-Action service-learning experiences are complex experiences with the students working together in groups to carry out a specific piece of the action plan. Because of this, different groups may be working on diverse aspects of the service-learning experience at the same time. The teacher, as the coordinator of the Community-Action experience, must be aware of what each group is doing at all times. Community-Action experiences are student-run and student-focused, but the teacher still needs to coordinate and oversee the actions taken by the students. The Weekly Action Report (see Chapter 5) completed by each group can help the teacher make sure every group is on track to meet its goals. In a Community-Action service-learning experience, the teacher's role should be one of facilitator rather than director. For instance, if the need occurs for certain groups to go off campus to perform research, present its ideas to a community organization, or carry out part of the action plan, the teacher needs to arrange for the field trip administratively; however, it is the students who should make contact with the service recipient or the community partner regarding what is to be done on the field trip. The teacher's role should be to facilitate the action as the students plan and carry out a viable action plan.

Community-Action and Critical Thinking

Community-Action, the highest level in this typology, corresponds to all six levels of Bloom's Taxonomy: Knowledge, Comprehension, Application, Analysis, Synthesis, and Evaluation. It also incorporates all four levels of Webb's Depth of Knowledge: Recall, Basic Application of Skill and Content, Strategic Thinking, and Extended Thinking. At the Community-Action level, students compile information in different ways by combining elements in a new pattern or proposing alternative solutions. They also present and defend opinions by making judgments and validating ideas or quality of work based on a set of criteria. Younger students participating at the Community-Action level of service should not be expected to advance developmentally beyond Bloom's Analysis level of critical thinking (see the Developmental Service-Learning Typology chart in Appendix B). Participating in their service-learning experience, most students at the Community-Action level might attempt to answer questions such as:

- What could be combined or modified to improve or change the situation?
- What actions did you take to overcome obstacles that occurred during the service-learning project?
- How would you predict the outcome if changes were made?
- Did the service recipients and community partners have different goals? How did you determine which objective(s) to incorporate into your action plan?
- How would you formulate a theory or construct a model that would change the way people perceive the situation?
- How did this service-learning experience impact the way you view the need area, the community, and yourself?
- What methods would you use to assess the value, importance, and success of your ideas and actions?
- Based on what you now know, how would you defend your decisions to others in the community including your community partners and the service recipients?
- What original methods did you create to convey information and complete your project?

Starter Ideas for Community-Action Activities

Because Community-Action experiences are more comprehensive and can involve a wider variety of actions, the first two ideas listed have been expanded to include potential curricular links. The expanded ideas include symbols that denote curriculum area connection (CC). LA represents language/arts; M represents math; SC represents science; SS represents social studies; A represents art; and CT represents computer technology. In order not to stifle teacher and student choice and voice, the remaining Community-Action list is composed of basic starter ideas without reference to a specific curricular connection.

This will allow you to adapt and expand the starter ideas to fit the content area and curriculum standards you teach and the needs of your students.

- Conduct an inventory of the parks, playgrounds, or other recreational areas in your community. Determine who uses these areas, the condition of the equipment and landscape, the amount of trash and debris, how safe the areas are for both children and adults, and other pertinent information. Choose a park or playground with serious concerns and begin brainstorming ways to improve the situation. Create and implement a plan of action to address the concerns of the area. Ideas to consider for your final plan of action should be amenable to your required curriculum standards. For instance, in a high-school physics class, it might be good to involve your students in raising money for new playground equipment after investigating safety concerns based on the physics behind each piece of equipment. A language arts class might concentrate on using letter-writing skills and/or writing newspaper articles about their project. A social studies class might consider conducting surveys to determine the nature of the problem and/or have local organizations, schools, or businesses work with the city parks and recreation department to "adopt" a park. A math class could write a grant to get new playground equipment, thereby developing mathematical skills. A special education class might investigate which playground equipment it prefers as well as equipment that is handicapped accessible. A computer technology class could use a CAD program to lay out the playground and the playground equipment. An art class could meet with a landscape architect in order to learn how to design walking trails and landscaping. Many other activities could be done to incorporate objectives in all content areas; one class could do multiple activities, thereby integrating many curricula objectives, not just the content objectives in which the class is taught (CC: LA, M, SC, SS, A, CT).

- Students could conduct a community-based survey to determine the level of crime and violence in the community (SS). After researching the types of crime and violence in the community, the students could create charts and graphs to illustrate their findings; they could also determine the percent of increase in crime over a number of years (M). After determining that crime is a significant issue in the community, the students could design and implement a campaign to reduce crime in their community (SS). They could write business letters to city and/or county officials asking for support as well as write a letter to the editor of the newspaper expressing their concerns and/or solution ideas (LA). They could design brochures to distribute within the community in order to increase public awareness of the issue (LA, A). They could design a webpage relating to crime-prevention strategies (CT). They could create a slideshow presentation and go to local clubs and organizations spreading their message (LA, A, CT, SS).

- Investigate land-use and green-space guidelines in your community. Petition city officials and/or private landowners to donate land to be used as a community nature trail and habitat for native plants, trees, and small animals. Research environmentally friendly options and work with interested parties to develop a plan to design, build, and maintain the trail and habitat.

- Investigate the percentage of those voting regularly in elections in your town or county. Research the reasons people don't go to the polls and vote. Publish your findings in the local newspaper. Brainstorm ways to increase the percentage of voters and create an effective plan of action to implement.

- Research your town history. Investigate historical buildings or sculptures in your community, being sure to take accurate measurements. Brainstorm ways to publicize and/or preserve your community's heritage. Work with community partners to implement your plan of action.

- Investigate homelessness in your school and community and chart your findings using graphs. Find out what types of resources are available and if those resources are used by those in need. Design and implement a plan to coordinate and/or expand the available resources.

- Survey literacy levels in your community and research the effects of illiteracy. Design and implement a literacy campaign to target specific needs in your school and/or community.

- Research the impact of peer pressure on learning in your school. Investigate methods of using positive peer pressure to encourage improved student behavior and increased interest in academics. Work with the PTA and school administrators to implement your plan of action.

- Conduct an environmental inventory of the land and water resources in your area. Learn how to test the soil and water at selected sites for pollutants. Investigate the cause of the pollution and target specific areas for cleanup.

- Find out the impact of budget cuts on your school. Survey your principal and teachers on most-needed supplies and create a priority list of needs. Design a plan to involve local businesses and community members in filling those needs.

- Investigate the causes and effects of bullying in your school. Research interventions and meet with your principal, student council, and PTA to suggest a plan to bully-proof your school.

- Investigate the impact of diversity issues on your school. Brainstorm ways to better understand the culture and customs of your schoolmates and teachers. Create and implement a plan both to appreciate diversity and benefit from the diversity.

- Study how waste is disposed of in your community. Investigate the support for recycling and/or reusing repairable items. Create a plan for recycling paper, cans, plastic, and reusable items in city offices and all schools. Develop incentives for local business to do the same.

- Research the causes and effects of acid rain and/or other forms of air pollution on the environment. Test levels in your community and publish your findings in the local newspaper. Design a community plan to monitor and reduce the air pollution.

- Investigate the level of the blood supply in your community. Create and implement a plan to encourage regular donors of all blood types.

- Research the level of drug and/or alcohol use in your school. Survey the student body to determine how and why they began taking drugs and/or using alcohol. Create a campaign to help them understand the dangers of substance abuse. Work with county health officials to plan safe and effective interventions to reduce usage.

- Take an awareness walk through your community looking for health and safety hazards. Interview the police and firemen about the most common safety hazards. Design and present a program for young children on the possible dangers and methods of prevention. Create a brochure for their parents on how to help protect them.

- Establish a connection between the generations by visiting with senior citizens, veterans, and older residents in their homes, hospitals, or nursing homes to offer companionship and record an oral history of past times for posterity. Develop a book of their insights to document and honor their wealth of knowledge and possibly sell as a fundraiser to benefit the seniors.

- Conduct an audit of the public and private transportation services available in your community. Determine if there is a need not being served, such as getting youth to extracurricular activities, seniors or the disabled to doctor appointments or grocery stores, or the unemployed to job opportunities. Create and implement a plan to make your town more accessible to all.

- Discover if your town has a problem with latchkey children. Investigate ways of providing a safe place where they can interact after school, do homework, and also learn new skills. Work with community partners to create a safe place for these children.

- Catalog and cross-reference all the nonprofit organizations and civic agencies in your county with the assistance they provide. Design and implement a plan to publicize all the services available, especially to new or needy residents. Recruit volunteers to offer information and assistance as needed.

The above-mentioned ideas are simply an overview of common community issues on which youth can take action. They may not apply to your community. It is important for youth to investigate concerns specific to the needs of their own community and that you connect their service-learning to a curriculum standard.

Examples of Community-Action Service-Learning

HARD ROCK Kids

"As you walk past the dilapidated Rock Gym in Elberton, the shattered, gloomy monument of Franklin D. Roosevelt stares at you—but not for long!" according to Jill Hamilton, a HARD ROCK Kid from Elberton, Georgia. The HARD ROCK Kids (HARD ROCK is an acronym for Having a Real Dream, Restoring Our Cultural Keepsakes) set out to survey monuments in their community as a part of SOS!, Save Outdoor Sculpture, a national organization dedicated to helping communities all over the United States learn about and preserve their public sculptures. The HARD ROCK Kids discovered that outdoor sculpture is the most accessible form of art and history found in most communities in the United States. Unfortunately, outdoor sculpture is a severely endangered cultural resource suffering from neglect, environmental pollution, and vandalism. These twelve-year-old students from Elbert County Middle School in Elberton, Georgia, found that people in their community didn't really appreciate these forms of art and had made no efforts to care for these sculptures.

From the monuments they surveyed, they found two that had significant damage, one from water damage and the other from vandalism. The one in most need of restoration was the monument of Franklin D. Roosevelt on the campus of their middle school. The historic monument was in six pieces and was badly chipped, with the face having taken the brunt of blows from a sledgehammer. Over a period of fifty-four years, the monument had been the victim of extreme vandalism. The other sculpture was atop the massive, abandoned Rock Gym. The Roosevelt monument was propped in front of the badly damaged gym. Bigger than the actual physical problem with the Rock Gym was the attitude of many of the people of the community concerning the gym. There was an effort underway to tear down the Rock Gym, a historic structure built by the Conservation Civilian Corps during the New Deal, and replace it with a parking lot.

The students began discussing the situation in class. They all felt that this was no way to treat the memory of such a great president as Franklin D. Roosevelt. After brainstorming solutions to their underlying challenge, the HARD ROCK Kids went to work to restore *their* monuments and tackle the problem of getting the community to restore the gym since one of their monuments was sitting over its doorway. Ultimately this group of middle-school students wrote and received a $12,000 grant to restore the FDR monument. Then they researched and wrote a historic nomination for the Rock Gym and included the two monuments in the nomination, as both were associated with the structure. The director of the state Department of Natural Resources Historic Preservation Division was impressed with their work and expressed how rare it was that a National Register nomination generated as much excitement as the Rock Gym nomination did. He found it refreshing and satisfying that young people were getting the message that we must preserve our important properties.

The students worked in groups to complete their tasks in language-arts class. They divided into two sets of groups: one for the service-learning part, the other for the historic nomination part. The service-learning groups that included everyone in the class were the Facilitators, Scrapbook, Correspondence, Media, Journalism, and Public Relations. The research groups, which also included everyone in the class, were the History Group, the Significance Group, the Description Group, the Art Group, and the Grant Group. Each group had its own plan book where the students created plans for the week and kept up with the action taken. On Fridays, they made plans for the following week and orally reported to the class what each group had done—their action taken—during the week. They created and used a star chart and earned stars for a reward at the end of the six-week reporting period. The Rock Gym ultimately received its historic recognition from the Department of the Interior, and many years later, it is being renovated. As one syndicated columnist remarked about her impression of the HARD ROCK Kids, "Chisel it in stone. When young people work, there will be progress" (Johnson 1995, B1).

Kelli's reflection concerning her work with one of the monuments follows:

> Most people don't really think much about monuments. Neither did I until I got involved with Save Outdoor Sculptures (SOS!). The first time I went to see the Elberton Granite Bicentennial Memorial Fountain, I thought that the monument was just a piece of granite, but now I know that the monument is sort of mine. Of course, it is everyone's monument. . . . [It] isn't just a symbol of our country, it is a true masterpiece. I think people should be more careful around all monuments because they are really our cultural keepsakes. Monuments are a part of everyone's heritage.

The level of this reflection is Synthesis.

This is Blair's reflection:

> How much do we actually know about our own heritage? How many people in Elbert County know that there is a sculpture above the entrance to the Old Rock Gym/Armory? Well, for those you who didn't know, there above the Old Rock Gym entrance rests the almost two-foot-tall and eight-foot-wide granite bird, the Phoenix. The Phoenix is in fair condition but is semi-covered with moss and with small amounts of cracking mortar around the bottom of the bird where the sculpture is attached to the gym. The Phoenix would definitely benefit from some cleaning and repair work, basically a large touch-up job. The problem with the Phoenix is that it's on the Old Rock Gym. This means that if the gym were to be torn down, the Phoenix would go with it. Well, maybe some people don't care about the Old Rock Gym and would be glad if it were to be torn down. Some people may think that it makes the school look ugly. Since it's condemned and no one uses it, why not tear it down and use it for a parking lot? Well, consider that it could be used for more classrooms for the school, a new band room, a new art room, and even a small community theater. I am aware that this would cost money and aware that these ideas are far into the future (or maybe not), but I think we should try to save the Old Rock Gym. Just imagine the possibilities for the gym. The Phoenix sits atop a magnificent, very sound structure hoping some day to return to her place of prominence. If a group of young students has its way, she just might rise out of the ashes to live for another period!

The level of this reflection is Analysis. Jill, one of the facilitators of the project, wrote the following reflection:

> As you walk past the dilapidated Rock Gym in Elberton, the shattered, gloomy monument of Franklin D. Roosevelt stares at you. This is the face of an admired president, the face of Franklin D. Roosevelt. Prezzi, the artist, designed this monument because he admired FDR and wanted to design a monument of him. While in the making,

Prezzi died, and Richard Cecchini finished the sculpture. On March 14, 1941, it was dedicated along with the Armory. The Franklin D. Roosevelt monument really needs some major work. . . . I would like to get together some kind of program to restore FDR. I would do it for Prezzi. Prezzi really did care for this monument to put forth such an effort to make this magnificent sculpture. I know that it is possible to restore FDR, and I know that I would be capable of leading the effort (with a little help). If anyone else is interested in the restoration of this project, please contact me. . . . I think that it is a shame that a monument to one of our greatest presidents, as well as one of Elbert County's cultural keepsakes, is in such a state of disrepair and despair.

The level of this reflection is Synthesis.

Focusing on the Learner Most of these students learned much more than they set out to learn when starting this assignment in a language-arts class. Initially they were just to survey outdoor sculptures in their community. They measured them, researched their history, and wrote an article for the local newspaper reporting their findings. But they did so much more because they began to care about the monuments and realized what they meant on a deeper level. They took action, and most of the students became passionately involved with the project, making a great difference in their community, although not all of the students were committed.

Thoughts to Ponder Not all students in this class became passionately involved with this project. Some surveyed their monuments and wrote very matter-of-fact articles about what they observed and discovered through research. As a teacher, you should expect this in your own class with your own Community-Action service-learning experiences. This is where differentiation strategies work well. For those students who want to continue and deepen their work, differentiation strategies give them that opportunity. This can be done through differentiation of content, process, and/or product in the classroom. For example, you could give students an opportunity to be exempt from regular classwork by offering them pretests of some material in the curriculum, through curriculum compacting, and/or through independent study.

If you notice, the excerpt from Blair's reflections are lengthier than Kelli's, but Kelli's reflection is assessed as a higher level of reflection, Synthesis. That may seem contraindicative until you examine the level of thinking that Kelli's writing represents compared with Blair's. Blair describes her monument and analyzes it well. She doesn't, however, go beyond the monument. Kelli looks beyond her monument and thinks more abstractly when she states, "Monuments are a part of everyone's heritage." Jill's reflections are also at the Synthesis level. Why? Because she has looked beyond the sculpture itself and connected with Prezzi, the immigrant sculptor who began his creation out of admiration for FDR and died before its completion. She saw beyond the monument itself into the heart of the sculptor. Kelli's and Jill's writings reflect a higher stage of cognitive development, Piaget's Formal Operational stage, whereas Blair's writing clearly reflects the lower Concrete Operational stage of cognitive development.

Horton's Helpers

> Imagine being able to distinguish a Corinthian column from an Ionic or Doric column. Imagine knowing the difference between Greek Revival, Gothic Revival, and Colonial Revival. Now imagine being able to distinguish these things at the age of eleven or twelve. With the motto, "Helping Horton is our concern," twenty-eight students at Horton County Middle School are taking their town by storm. Dubbing themselves the [Horton's] Helpers, these seventh-grade students have become experts on the history and architecture of their small town, and they are taking their expertise to the streets. (Joiner 1999, 1)

This service-learning project involved partnering with a town in a rural area in the South. From decorating the downtown during the holidays to coordinating the Main Street Monster Mash, a carnival event that brought trick-or-treaters safely to the downtown on Halloween for treats and fun activities, the students, Horton's Helpers, helped with activities designed to get people to frequent the downtown. They also researched historic buildings and homes in Horton, educated the community, and designed a walking tour of the area, which included twenty-four stops. In addition to the walking tours, the students designed brochures, eventually putting the information on CD for easy reference.

The students began to discern new meaning in the term *community*; to value involvement in the community, both "seeing" the town's history and taking pride in it; to feel responsibility toward the community; to acknowledge the importance of enjoying one's work; and to recognize real-world motivations for community involvement by adults, which can be self-serving. The students went from taking their community for granted in the beginning to "seeing" it for the first time. Cooperative skills were enhanced—how to work as a team, how to get along with people in a group, and how to respect others' points of view. Through their participation in this project, the students began to see outside the walls of their classroom into the community beyond. As their community horizons expanded, their appreciation of their community and political efficacy grew.

The African American students recognized that they had experienced the service-learning project differently. One stated, "I'm like the only black girl in there. . . . [I]t was kinda [sic] different because I didn't have any friends, cuz [sic] I was kinda [sic] shy in my other classes, you know. And, but, we kinda [sic] get closer. . . . We're all pretty, uh, equal now." Bryan, another African American, expressed similar feelings, also using the word *equal* to relate how he felt from participating in the project. They were the only students to reference feelings of equality. This indicates that working in close cooperation with others toward a common goal in the community could prove to be effective in bridging the chasm that still exists between the races in some areas of the South.

This project had both a direct and an indirect impact on the community. Directly, it led to beautification of the downtown area, the education of the community about its historic resources, and the involvement of more people in the downtown. It also had an indirect impact on the community. Viewing youth as a positive element in the community was one effect of the project. Another involved student attitudes. As one student related, by knowing more about your community, you learn to like your community better, which gives you a reason to stay involved in the future.

The methodology used in the service-learning class was important. Working cooperatively using the creative problem solving process and the cognitive apprenticeship framework was important. Because the students were given *choice* and *voice* in selecting the project based on their assessment of problems and needs in the community, commitment to it was enhanced. Celebration was represented in this service-learning experience by the students being selected to exhibit and demonstrate their project in the Community Problem-Solving Fair at the Future Problem Solving Program's International Conference. They shared their work with teams of students from around the world. This participation enhanced the attitudes, student development, and commitment.

The following reflections were captured in interviews with a researcher doing a study on the project. The first interview was with one of the facilitators (leaders) in the class and captures the structure of the class.

Interviewer: First of all, tell me about your job as facilitator.
Laura: What I have to do is, like, okay, everybody in the room has a job, like, some people are in the media center, I mean, the media group; others, like the correspondence group and publicity group and stuff like that. And so, like, when we're working on stuff, I had to walk around and make sure that everybody is, like, doing things, and I like that.

Interviewer: Well, they seem to listen to you. Has it helped you in having this role [as facilitator (leader) of the project] to develop those skills?

Laura: Yeah, um, like, when I came to sixth grade, I was kinda shy. . . . Mrs. Smith helped us work on our talking skills. That's not exactly what she called it, but we had to read stuff and she would have us write papers and stuff, and she thought I was a pretty good writer so she let me write things and I'd read them in front of the class, and it made it easier for me to talk to people because I used to be real shy.

The next segment is taken from an interview with Bryan, one of the African American members of Horton's Helpers, about what his experience as a Horton's Helper meant to him, which reflects the highest level of reflection, Synthesis.

You know, like I said, I haven't been really part of anything, and this is the only thing I have been part of, and I had to work as a team now besides baseball and rec [recreation league]. . . . We work good together, you know. We have our ups and downs sometimes . . . is normal. But all this debating going on, you get to learn more about each other. . . . [Y]ou know, they [Horton's Helpers] treated you equal like your brothers and sisters would. That's why, one of the reasons I like being in the [Horton's Helpers], 'cause [sic] of the respect you get from the other members.

Focusing on the Learner Written by students after a field trip to the cemetery to do research, the next reflections illustrate how students involved in the same service-learning experience can reflect at different levels. The first reflection is an Observation-level reflection.

I thought our trip to the cemetery was fun and made us think. Lots of war veterans were buried there. They were mostly young, too. There were other graves in the cemetery, too. The oldest person was over a hundred years old! The youngest person buried there was born and died on the same day. That was sad. Who knew a trip to a graveyard could be so interesting.

For Aaron, his community began to take on a life of its own, a life that needed sustaining by its citizens. His Synthesis-level reflections get to the heart of Community-Action service-learning.

I thought a community would be fine by itself and then after getting into this, it's, like, I didn't realize how much it really needs. At the cemetery, a lot of the tombstones and everything are just decaying away—[there will] come a time when you won't even be able to tell—we'd be losing our history. Our history is there. If our monuments aren't being preserved, they're just going to eventually rot away, and this is a part of our history.

Thoughts to Ponder What if the teacher of this class had guided the student reflections by asking the students questions based on higher levels of reflection instead of just asking the students to write about their experience? Questions like the ones that follow might have triggered more thoughtful responses:

- How does what you learned from the cemetery experience connect with the history of Horton that we have learned about through our service-learning project?

- How could we connect the cemetery experience to the walking tours being planned?

- How might inclusion of the cemetery in the walking tour make people connect better to their past?

Ask the Experts

1. *My school system recently sponsored a system-wide service-learning workshop. One of the speakers mentioned something he called the Essential Elements. What are they? Can you explain where Community-Action fits in relation to these Essential Elements?*

Learn and Serve America's National Service-Learning Cooperative, a group of thirteen organizations funded by the Corporation for National and Community Service in order to provide assistance and expertise in the area of service-learning throughout the United States, put together what it termed the *Essential Elements of Service-Learning* (Toole 1998). The essential elements highlight the structural components of four levels of service-learning, which includes teaching and organizational benchmarks that describe successful service-learning practice. The outcomes of Community-Action service-learning correspond with Level IV, the highest level, of the Essential Elements of Service-Learning. For example, corresponding to Level IV of the first essential element in the cluster labeled Cluster I: Learning, during these projects there are multiple learner outcomes that exceed and spread beyond the boundaries of the curriculum. During their participation in Community-Action service-learning, students apply higher-order thinking skills and promote dialogue and understanding among a diverse audience while often reaching both local and state curriculum objectives as well. As outlined in Level IV, students participating at the Community-Action level are stretched in all ways in their learning and are able to identify external and internal factors that impose limits upon them as well as being able to devise means to overcome these boundaries. If you look through the various Level IV clusters on the Essential Elements of Service-Learning, which is downloadable from the website of the Northwest Regional Education Laboratory as a PDF file (see "Service-Learning Resources" in Appendix B), you will see many connections between the desired elements of Level IV and Community-Action service-learning.

2. *I understand the theory behind offering students more choice and voice in the selection and implementation of a Community-Action project, but in actuality, it seems as if things work more smoothly, take less time, and have a clearer connection to the curriculum if I just assign the project and related tasks. I have assigned projects for the past two years, and we have done some very good work in our community. Why should I change now?*

You have hit on a very important concept. If you address service-learning from the standpoint of the teacher, your method seems appropriate. If, however, you address service-learning from the standpoint of the learner, it is not appropriate. Giving students a choice and voice as well as allowing them to be the action takers in a project promotes more excitement and commitment among the students because they feel more ownership and leadership of the project. This stretches their thinking and extends their learning as they take on real-life roles and responsibilities that challenge them to grow cognitively, socially, and emotionally. By offering your students choices for the project focus from among a variety of curriculum-related ideas, you can still ensure a connection to your curriculum without assigning a specific service-learning experience. As a teacher, it is also sometimes difficult to *fade* and let the students be the ones who take the action. Although it may seem quicker and easier to do it yourself, more learning takes place when you encourage and allow your students to become the decision makers and to learn how to apply higher-order thinking skills in authentic situations. Your role should be to facilitate, to support, and to encourage your students as they select, plan, and implement the action. Three of the five components of the Best-Practice Model for Community-Action Service-Learning—the cognitive apprenticeship model, cooperative learning strategies, and creative problem solving—work together to help you become the *guide on the side* while your students become empowered to make a difference in the real world.

3. *Seeing that Community-Action is the highest level on your typology, it seems like it is valued more than the other levels. Is this the case?*

Community-Action is the highest level on the typology because it promotes more positive outcomes for both the student and the community than the other levels of service-learning. The teacher, however, should place the most value on whichever level of service-learning he or she determines is the most appropriate for his or her students. The type of service-learning teachers decide to do should be determined by a number of factors, not the least of which is the developmental level of their students. As with any type of pedagogy teachers employ, the first consideration is the curriculum content. What are the objectives? How will service-learning help the students reach these content and skill objectives? How much time can be given to the service-learning experience? Generally speaking, the higher the level of service-learning, the greater the time commitment.

References

Alliance for Service Learning in Education Reform. 1993. *Standards of Quality and Excellence for School-Based Service Learning.* Washington, DC: Council of Chief State School Officers.

Bradley, James. 1995. "A Model for Evaluating Student Learning in Academically Based Service." In *Connecting Cognition and Action: Evaluation of Student Performance in Service Learning Courses,* edited by M. Troppe, 13–26. Providence, RI: Campus Compact.

Brown, John Seely, Allan Collins, and Paul Duguid. 1989. "Situated Cognition and the Culture of Learning." *Educational Researcher* 18 (1): 32–42.

Henderson, Bruce. 1987. "The Kids Who Saved a Dying Town." *Reader's Digest,* September, 42–46.

Johnson, Rheta Grimsley. 1995. "Hard Rock Kids Are as Good as Granite." *The Atlanta Journal and The Atlanta Constitution,* January 8, B1.

Joiner, K. 1999. "Walking Through History. . . ." *Serving to Learn* 1 (2): 1–9.

Osborn, Alex. 1963. *Creative Imagination.* 3rd ed. New York: Charles Scribner.

Parnes, Sidney. 1967. *Creative Behavior Guidebook.* New York: Charles Scribner.

Piaget, Jean. 1950. *The Psychology of Intelligence.* San Diego: Harcourt Brace Jovanovich.

Slavin, Robert E. 1986. "Cooperative Learning: Engineering Social Psychology in the Classroom." In *The Social Psychology of Education: Current Research and Theory,* edited by R. S. Feldman. Cambridge: Cambridge University.

Toole, Pamela, ed. 1998. *Essential Elements of Service-Learning.* St. Paul, MN: National Youth Leadership Council.

Torrance, E. Paul. 1995. *Why Fly?* Norwood, NJ: Ablex Publishing Corporation.

Webb, Norman. 1999. "Alignment of Science and Mathematics Standards and Assessments in Four States: Research Monograph No. 18."

Chapter Five

Implementing Service-Learning in the Classroom

The SWaMP Kids: Looking at Service-Learning Through a Developmental Lens

> When kids talk trash, this town listens. Teachers say it's a constructive use of time. Officials say it saves them money. The SwaMP Kids, a group of sixth- and seventh-graders tackling some of Franklin County's toughest solid-waste problems, say they are just like any garbage consultants except for one thing. "We're a whole lot cheaper," said Todd Ray, thirteen. Their latest assignment is a ten-year solid-waste plan the northeast Georgia county must submit to state officials by July 1. (Franklin Co. "Green Gang" Kids Talk Trash and Save Their County Money 1993, 3)

Starting out as a simple recycling Community-Service service-learning project, the project conducted by the SWaMP Kids morphed over time, culminating in a Community-Action service-learning project, a project that created very dramatic results in their community. Over a period of three years, these students went through all three developmental stages of service-learning, beginning with Community-Service, then to Community-Exploration, and finally to Community-Action.

The students ultimately wrote a 750-page, state-approved Solid Waste Management Plan for their county, which prevented their county landfill from closing. The project earned the group a Presidential Environmental Youth Award, and several of the students were guests on an episode of the *Donahue Show* highlighting kids who have made a difference.

Most of the students involved in the SwaMP project carried out their work daily in a middle-school classroom. SWaMP, an acronym for Solid Waste Management Plan, appeared on the students' class schedules. The basic structure of the SWaMP class was based on Brown, Collins, and Duguid's (1989) theory of cognitive apprenticeship, which describes four elements that lead to learning. The first element, scaffolding, takes place when the more-knowledgeable other scaffolds the learner's performance of a task, acting as a crutch until the learner can perform the task alone. Next is modeling, when the learner watches the more-knowledgeable other. Then comes the coaching, as the more-knowledgeable other stays involved, encouraging the learner and offering reminders. The final element is the fading, when the more-knowledgeable other gradually fades from the task, taking down the scaffolding, until the learner is actually doing the task independently.

Observing the SWaMP Kids in their classroom, one couldn't help but note the uniqueness of the Community-Action service-learning class concerning the division of labor and the way the students were organized into groups to work on different parts of the project.

> The seventh-graders work on the project daily, dividing up the tasks of gathering different information. Joni Childs has been puzzling over financing tactics such as sales taxes and enterprise funds, while Katie Norris has been crunching numbers on recyclables and garbage volume. (McCarthy 1993, D1)

Katie, one of the SWaMP Kids, reflected on the methodology that was used during her service-learning experience:

> And I think any community project basically has the same structure. . . . You identify a problem, come up with a possible solution, and, a bunch of possible solutions—the best possible solution . . . I think we used that throughout the plan. . . . You know, here's our problem; these are all our solutions. Which one's the best? Which one's going to impact our community the best? You knew what you had to do. We each had a teacher planner book that we had to fill out for the week. . . . It [the class] wasn't structured at all, but we knew what we had to do. (Terry 2000, 123)

Formal reflection was central to this Community-Action service-learning experience, as it is with most highly effective service-learning experiences. Each group utilized a plan book, listing both its goals for the week and its accomplishments. A journal, a timeline, and a scrapbook were maintained, which advanced the reflective process. Also, the SWaMP Kids gathered together during their regular class time, usually once a week, to share what they had worked on, what hurdles they had encountered, and what their accomplishments had been.

After attending a workshop in a nearby urban area, the SWaMP Kids had a discussion about what they had experienced. They discussed the information they had learned about recycling, garbage trucks, composting, and landfills. They learned such terms as *think locally* and *low tech*. They laughingly concluded that their county was closer to *no tech* than *low tech*.

Talk-show host Phil Donahue was very impressed with what the SWaMP Kids had accomplished. When several of the SWaMP Kids appeared on the *Donahue Show*, he expressed wonderment that a group of teens could accomplish what they had in their community:

> Think about this! These are teenagers. . . . Imagine the consciousness now, the awareness at age fourteen. They'll have it all their lives. These folks are not going to pollute; they're not going to waste. They're going to recycle, and they're going to make a better world, not only for us, but for themselves and their children as well. You have our congratulations! (Wheeler 1994)

Katie's comments about what she learned from the SWaMP project seemed to speak to the essence of cooperation. She was the facilitator—the leader—of the group, and sometimes there were problems with others in the class. When this occurred, Katie would become very frustrated. The others, however, would become just as frustrated— *with her*.

> [I learned] a lot of teamwork and that no two people are really alike, but if you deal with the differences it's all going to all turn out. I mean, me and [Laura] hated each other—I mean hated with a capital H—we hated each other! And yet I had an amount of respect for her, and she had an amount of respect for me simply because we had to work together. . . . Through teamwork, I learned to just tolerate people—not like 'em [sic]—not really care if they drop off the face of the earth, but tolerate them! I used to just blow up at people. . . . I guess we were working in such close quarters that, you know, if somebody that you didn't like was there, they were going to breathe on you at some point. You were going to have to put up with it. (Terry 2000, 126–27)

When most of school is controlled for students, it is not too difficult to understand why personal commitment is often missing in schools. Service-learning projects such as this one conducted by the SWaMP Kids promote caring and commitment. The SWaMP Kids felt it; they lived it; they expressed it.

During their project, when they were confronted with overwhelming problems that accompany most solid-waste issues, especially the costs involved, the SWaMP Kids did not quiver. The local paper reported, "But that [the costs and problems] didn't temper the enthusiasm of the students, who seem to realize that they are the future. 'We hope that we can be the difference that will get through to the citizens of Franklin County,'" ("Students Have Ideas for Landfill" 1991, 13) was the response of one of the SWaMP Kids. And due to their unwavering commitment, they were.

Years later, SWaMP Kid Katie went head to head with Fieldale Farms Corporation, a large poultry company. She was instrumental in preventing a poultry by-product sludge dumping site from locating in her community. She also has helped another group of citizens near her college fight a regional landfill development plan.

The SWaMP Kids became empowered to make a difference in their community. They loved being treated *like adults*. "Kids can make a difference!" ("Way to Go!" 1994, 129), exclaimed one SWaMP Kid who was a finalist in the Noxzema Extraordinary Teen Contest for her role in the project. And that difference is so incredibly exciting to the students.

When students begin projects like these, they are unable to realize the far-reaching effects these service-learning experiences can have. As Katie expressed, "We [SWaMP Kids] knew what we were doing, and we knew the potential of the project—although we never thought we'd actually get that far." As it was with the SWaMP Kids, by the end of service-learning experiences like these, students often feel they can conquer the world. Katie articulated it this way:

> I think we got an early glimpse of what a career is really like because . . . *we* had a personal interest in what *we* were writing. . . . I think that that in itself made us all realize that we were doing something kinda [sic] ahead of our time, yet we were doing a good job at it. And, for me, it was, like, hey, this is what having a job's really like. And for *us*, I think it was like having a job that you love and you have a personal interest in. And, as seventh-graders, I mean, none of our friends had any clue—you know? I look back on that, and they were still listening to New Kids on the Block and starting to dye their hair, and we're trying to save Franklin County and . . . we really got an early glimpse. (Terry 2000, 134)

A Developmental Approach to Service-Learning

Considering a developmental approach to service-learning (see the Developmental Service-Learning Typology in Appendix B), the question arises: is one service activity better than another? Isn't students setting up a recycling program in their school, as the students mentioned above did initially, considered a low level of service-learning? Should this type of activity even be considered service-learning? Using a developmental approach to service-learning, the answer is yes. This type of service-learning is appropriate when using a developmental model for less mature students who have never participated in service-learning or for students at a lower cognitive developmental stage. After all, you wouldn't try to teach algebra to first graders, would you? No, you would first teach them basic math skills, building on those until they were ready developmentally to comprehend the abstractness of algebra.

Why should service-learning be different? If our goal is to focus on the learner, then shouldn't we adjust our lens to include a developmental view of service-learning? Does this mean that Community-Service service-learning should be accepted as a pathway to higher levels of service-learning? Just like basic math paves the way to more advanced concepts of algebra, basic levels of service-learning pave the way to more advanced levels of service-learning.

No one is advocating that service-learning should ever be disconnected from the curriculum; to the contrary, service-learning activities should always be tied to the curriculum. It is difficult, however, to imagine that service-learning cannot relate to curriculum goals everywhere at all grade levels, especially since the National Council for the Social Studies defines social studies as "the integrated study of the social sciences and humanities to promote civic competence" (National Council for the Social Studies 2006). What better way to promote civic competence than through service-learning? And what better way to reach character-education objectives than through service-learning? The point is that simply aligning service-learning to curriculum objectives does not guarantee quality service-learning. In order to ascertain the quality of service-learning students are experiencing, one must focus on the learner and the level of his or her cognitive processing during the service-learning experience. Students, following a developmental approach, would progress from simple group projects in early years, as the SWaMP Kids did, through increasingly complex sequences as they learn skills of service and assume greater responsibility for initiating, planning, and carrying out service-learning experiences (Schine 1997).

We need to look beyond isolated service experiences and implement a sequential approach to service-learning. The developmental service-learning typology provides a much-needed developmental framework for classifying service-learning based on the developmental level of the learner. Students can proceed from the first level, Community-Service, which corresponds to Piaget's third stage of cognitive development, through the third level, Community-Action, which most often corresponds to Piaget's fourth stage of cognitive development. It also provides educators with an effective model for program development. By categorizing service-learning based on the developmental level of the learner—not just on where it takes place or how it is integrated into the curriculum—as well as understanding the types and outcomes associated with each level, we should be able to incorporate service-learning more effectively into K–12 classrooms.

Linking Service-Learning to the Curriculum

Teachers often ask how they can implement service-learning into their classroom. Many view service-learning as an add-on, something else they have to do in addition to what they are already doing. However, teachers should not consider service-learning as one more thing for them to do. They should view service-learning as a pedagogy, a method of teaching the content to their students. As with any pedagogy, teachers must start by developing curriculum objectives for what they are teaching. After developing the objectives they plan to address through the pedagogy of service-learning, they should then address what degree of service-learning suits their objectives, their students' needs, and the time they have to spend on teaching the objectives. In addition to addressing their content objectives, many teachers also turn to character-education objectives, which fit hand in hand with service-learning.

Service-Learning as a Differentiated Curriculum

A growing challenge for teachers today is differentiating instruction to respond to the needs of the diverse students in typical, inclusive, mixed-ability classrooms. There are multiple ways in the classroom to create a better fit for more learners. Adjustments based on learning profiles encourage students to understand their own learning preferences. In general, according to Tomlinson (1999), interest-based adjustments allow students to have a voice in their learning.

Characteristics that shape teaching and learning in an effective differentiated classroom fit beautifully with service-learning. In both methods, instruction is concept focused and principle driven. All students have the opportunity to explore and apply the key concepts of the subject being studied, and they have the opportunity to explore meaningful ideas through a variety of avenues and approaches. Both methods allow for consistent flexible grouping and for students to be active explorers. The teacher role in both is to facilitate, or guide, the exploration, and students learn to be responsible for their own learning. Not only does such student-centeredness give students more ownership of their learning but it also facilitates growing independence in thought, planning, and evaluation.

Service-learning lends itself well to differentiation in the classroom, particularly at the highest level of service-learning. Because Community-Action service-learning is so comprehensive, it provides multiple opportunities to differentiate the curriculum through process, product, content, and assessment. An outline of ways Community-Action service-learning provides opportunities to differentiate in the classroom is described in the following sections.

Process

Service-learning experiences provide multiple opportunities to explore ideas through the varied modalities: visual, kinesthetic, auditory, spatial, musical, and so on. The process can vary by group, service-learning topic, and strategy (ie. creative problem solving, inquiry, discovery, cooperative learning).

- Facilitator Group—oversees project and consults with groups
- Media Group—conducts interviews, writes articles, and conducts press conferences
- Correspondence Group—maintains community contacts and creates all correspondence
- Public Relations Group—creates art, advertising, and slogans; conducts fundraising
- Documentation Group—performs record keeping, videography, and photography
- Research Group(s)—utilizes traditional research and discovery techniques and makes use of primary sources

Product

The products produced vary by group and job responsibility and are dependent upon group and project goals:

- Media Group—produces articles, interviews, and speeches
- Public Relations Group—creates brochures, advertisements, and packaging events/promotions
- Documentation Group—makes videos, photographs, scrapbook, journal, and digital products
- Correspondence Group—writes letters, press releases, and invitations

Content

- The content in a service-learning experience is connected to the *real* world.
- Students self-select the service-learning focus through choice and voice and apply key principles to solve problems and extend their understandings.
- Students use varied materials based on individual readiness, group participation, and service-learning goals.
- Students work on different tasks in order to make sense of key ideas at varied levels of complexity.
- Service-learning features interrelated and cross-disciplinary studies.

Assessment

Service-learning provides opportunities for students to rethink ideas and reflect on information so that they can draw on key skills and understandings needed for the mastery of required curriculum objectives. Students work at different paces and are assessed according to varied group goals. Some methods of assessment include the following:

- Portfolios
- Weekly group reports
- Self-assessment based on individual goal setting
- Reflection rubrics
- Outcome/product
- Record keeping

Tools, Techniques, and Activities

This section introduces you to tools, techniques, and activities that have been found to foster quality service-learning. Each segment begins with a brief description followed by suggested activities and tools designed to encourage competency in that area. Many of the activities can be helpful at all levels of service-learning. Some are more appropriate for the higher levels of service-learning. Full-size handout masters related to each activity can be found in Appendix A. You will find the initials CS, CE, and/or CA at the bottom of each handout in Appendix A. These initials indicate the level of service-learning for which the activity is most appropriate:

- CS = Community-Service
- CE = Community-Exploration
- CA = Community-Action

Creative Problem Solving

Creative problem solving is a method of thinking and learning that takes a previously unsolved problem and analyzes it using both divergent (creative) and convergent (critical) thinking skills in order to arrive at a solution to the problem. Creative problem solving was introduced into the schools in 1974 when Dr. E. Paul Torrance adapted the Osborn-Parnes Creative Problem Solving Model (Osborn 1963; Parnes 1967) used in business for classroom use. This model is based on the following steps:

- Identifying problems and challenges
- Recognizing and stating the important problem
- Producing alternative solutions
- Evaluating alternative solutions
- Planning to put the solutions into use (Torrance 1995)

Why Is Creative Problem Solving Important in Service-Learning?

The creative problem solving process helps to structure the service-learning experience by providing logical steps for the students to follow from their initial investigation of community concerns to the implementation of their action plan. Creative problem solving also affords students the opportunity to acquire divergent and convergent thinking skills by giving them the opportunity to generate multiple options and then evaluate those options in order to decide on the better option(s). Students involved in higher levels of service-learning go beyond the creative problem solving planning stage and actually implement their solution ideas in the community.

Brainstorming is the most commonly used *divergent* thinking technique. It is used to identify issues and generate solution ideas. Brainstorming is a group problem solving technique that involves the spontaneous contribution of ideas from all members of the group. Quantity is desired when brainstorming as is "hitchhiking" on an idea—expanding on a basic idea contributed by a group member to create a new idea. Encourage a free flow of ideas among your students by creating masters of brainstorming starter ideas using computer graphics. Select a fun graphic that represents a common object that can be interpreted in many different ways. Print the graphic under an appropriate title on transparency film to use on an overhead projector or on plain paper to use as a handout. For instance, a graphic of a boomerang under the title of Things that Return . . . will probably generate a wide variety of responses from bouncing balls, library books, and movie sequels to letters without postage and the swallows of Capistrano to more abstract ideas like smiles, love, and good or bad deeds. Becoming comfortable with generating ideas by responding to the basic, fun brainstorming graphics should encourage your students to risk brainstorming creative ideas within their service-learning groups and to begin to view issues from many different perspectives, thereby increasing their fluency (quantity of ideas) and flexibility (variety of ideas).

While an evaluation matrix (see Appendix A) is an effective *convergent* thinking tool, in service-learning, focusing is often done either by general consensus of the class or by the "bean" method. The bean method involves giving each student ten to fifteen dry beans and allowing him or her to "spend" as many beans as he or she would like on any of the options—the option(s) with the highest number of beans win(s). The students' plan of action will differ depending on the level of service-learning you have chosen for the class. Using the creative problem solving process to help analyze the situation, make decisions, and plan the action is important, especially in the higher levels of service-learning.

Brainstorming—As Easy as 1, 2, 3!

Brainstorming can be somewhat threatening to students who are accustomed to answering a question with a textbook-supplied phrase. Once students realize that ideas that go beyond the obvious are not only acceptable but also encouraged, their creative juices begin flowing! The following steps can be helpful in teaching brainstorming to your students:

1. Introduce brainstorming to your students by showing them a transparency made from the Abstract Shape brainstorming master located in Appendix A. Ask the students what the shape on the overhead looks like to them. After you have gathered a variety of answers, turn the transparency 90 degrees to the right. Ask the students to brainstorm what they see in the design now. Keep turning the transparency and garnering responses from the students until you return the shape to the original position. Discuss how things can change when the same person views something from a different perspective as well as how different people can view the same thing differently. This activity is designed to help the students view things from different perspectives and value others' points of view.

2. Create transparencies of general brainstorming starter ideas. Some suggestions for starter idea masters include a graphic of: a boomerang for Things that Return . . . ; a bumblebee for Things that Bug You . . . ; a traffic light for Things that Change . . . : darts in a target for Things that Stick . . . ; the sun for Things that are Bright . . . ; balloons for Things that Go Up . . . ; trees for Things that Grow . . . ; and a brick wall for Things that are Hard. . . . Select a transparency and place it on the overhead. As a whole-group activity, ask the class to brainstorm ideas related to the transparency. All responses are *correct*, but there may be a few students who go beyond the obvious and offer a more abstract response to the graphic on the master. Once the first student mentions a *different* idea and it is received positively, it usually starts a chain reaction in which the other students also risk stating the less obvious, more creative responses. Sometimes middle-level students become so caught up in brainstorming that they come up with ideas that may be relevant to the topic but not appropriate for a classroom discussion. One way to handle this is to impose the *Grandmother Rule*—if their idea is inappropriate to say in front of their grandmother, it's inappropriate in the classroom. This simple guideline has been very effective in limiting off-color or inhumane ideas during brainstorming. The next step is to introduce the students to the Idea Jot Board (see Appendix A) and have them brainstorm ideas to the other brainstorming starter ideas on the Idea Jot Board in groups of four to six students.

3. When the students have become comfortable with the brainstorming process, select an everyday problem in which the students may be interested. Some general topic suggestions are: selecting a theme for a dance; deciding on a class field trip; improving the food in the cafeteria; choosing a service-learning topic. Either hand out a copy of the appropriate jot board to each group or use a transparency of the jot board. This will help the students become familiar with brainstorming both problem ideas (Challenges Jot Board) and solution ideas (Action Ideas Jot Board) to the selected concern (see Appendix A for all jot board masters).

What Is a Jot Board?

A jot board is a brainstorming tool that helps groups generate a multitude of ideas together—it is a place where ideas are created and quickly jotted down. Using a jot board involves the following points:

- Place a jot board in the middle of a group of four to six students. Simple phrases or drawings are fine on a jot board. The idea is to have all the students capture their ideas on the jot board at the same time, so some of the phrases may even be written upside down on the jot board.

- What is most important is that the students work together to brainstorm ideas related to the situation presented and record their ideas on the jot board.

- You know the jot board is being used correctly when students are leaning over it and making quite a mess on it—a mess where ideas flourish. If the group is noisy and pencils are moving, you know the jot board is working. A nebula is the birthplace of stars; a jot board is the birthplace of ideas.

Choice and Voice Techniques

Allowing the students to have a choice and voice in service-learning activities helps to ensure more interest in the project. The more choice and voice the students are given, the more interested and involved they will become. This involvement not only makes the students feel that their input is meaningful and valued but also encourages the development of leadership skills, planning, and personal responsibility. Think about it. What choices are students usually given in school? Not many. Service-learning gives students more opportunities to make choices and have their voices heard. Some ideas for providing choice and voice include:

- Allow the students to select the service-learning project idea.

- Allow students to conduct their own research around their interests.

- If this is a group service-learning experience, design action groups based on different intelligences and interests and then allow the students to choose their own groups. Ideas for groups are Facilitators, Media, Public Relations, Documentation, Correspondence, as well as Art, Technology, and other project-related groups.

- Providing opportunities for reflection is essential in service-learning. Giving students a voice in how they relate their reflections can lead to higher levels of reflection. Whereas some students may enjoy just writing about the experience through journaling techniques, others may prefer other means such writing poetry, singing a song they wrote, role-playing what they have done, or creating a slide presentation.

- Some service-learning activities may involve students doing presentations to those outside the classroom. If this is the case, allow the students to create their own presentations.

Any chance you have to allow the students to express their own voice and make their own choice, we advise you to take it. Please be sure to read through the activities in this section as well as the choice and voice handout masters in Appendix A.

Providing Choice and Voice in Exploration of the Community

Both while you are deciding on the service-learning topic and afterward, when you are finding out about the selected topic, research can provide multiple opportunities for choice and voice. Let the students have a voice in what specifically needs researching. Then allow them to select the part of the research in which they wish to be involved. Let them choose their own research groups. The assignment of each research group should be to discover information about the topic. What can they find out about the topic? How much of a problem is this area of concern in their community? How much interest is generated during the research part of this assignment?

To find the answers, the students might want to interview the teachers or students in their school, survey community members, check the archives of the local newspaper(s), or conduct research using Internet resources. By connecting their findings to the community concern, each research group should be able to determine how relevant the issue is to their community. At the conclusion of the initial research phase, each group reports its findings to the class. Letting each group decide how it will report gives further voice to the students. Some may just want to read a report. Others may want to use technology such as slideshow presentations, while others may want to use charts or other tools to share their results. Student choice and voice should be encouraged during the ongoing research that may be involved in the higher levels of service-learning.

What's in a Name?

A group identity and unity is often established within a group or class by encouraging the service-learning students to choose an acronym or a name for the group and/or the project.

Inform the class that they are going to select a name for the group and/or project in order to establish their identity with the community. Selecting a name can be accomplished as follows:

- As a class, have them brainstorm all the things that they associate with their service-learning activity or themselves so far.
- Record each idea on an overhead of the Idea Jot Board—no matter how far out it may seem.

- Circle the three or four names that the class likes the best.
- Have the class think about each of the circled names.
- Ask them to think of what each letter in the word or words could stand for that relates to the group and/or the service-learning experience.
- Have the class choose the name they think best represents their topic and their service-learning experience.

For example, a group of students who rescued their dying downtown chose RIPPLES, which is an acronym for Royston Involvement Project by Pupils for Lifting Economy and Society. Another group, who inventoried and restored an outdoor sculpture and successfully nominated the sculpture and the building where it was located for the Historic Register, selected HARD ROCK Kids for their identity. HARD ROCK is an acronym for Having A Real Dream, Restoring Our Cultural Keepsakes. Though not an acronym, another group of students who helped in the restoration of a historic theater in their community selected a name descriptive of their project, dubbing themselves The Backstage Crew.

Understanding the Job-Selection Process

Organization is the key to successful Community-Action service-learning. The first step in getting organized is to set up the working groups, so that the many project tasks are shared between the groups and don't seem so overwhelming. It is recommended that all students be assigned to a Research Group that will investigate various aspects of the community concern. Each student will also belong to one Action Group. In addition to the selected Action Group, several students may also volunteer to take on the jobs of Press Secretary, File Clerk, Digital Coordinator, Journalist, or Scrapbook Coordinator. The Facilitators, who should be elected by the class, should not take on any other responsibilities. Examples of major Action Groups follow:

- Facilitator's Action Group
- Correspondence Action Group
- Documentation Action Group
- Media Action Group
- Public Relations Action Group
- Topic-specific Action Groups, as needed

Copies should be made of the Job Selection form in Appendix A. The students should decide which group they would like to join. Job

Descriptions are also located in Appendix A. They should be photo-copied and given to the students or posted so that the students can read about the responsibilities and choose the job(s) they might want. You should then examine their job selection choices and try to put them in a group of their choosing.

Each group will vary in size, depending on the size of your class. The Facilitator's Group should have no more than three, preferably two; the Media, Correspondence, and Topic-specific Action Groups should have no more than four; the Documentation and Public Relations groups will be the largest groups, as their responsibilities are more entailed. Preferably one, and no more than two, is recommended for the jobs of Digital Coordinator, File Clerk, Journalist, and Scrapbook Coordinator. Depending upon your teaching objectives, the jobs can be alternated during the course of the service-learning experience so that each student can experience different roles and responsibilities.

There is *not* a choice for the Facilitator's Group on the Job Selection form. This is because the facilitators are elected to their positions by the class prior to other job selections. Therefore, there is no need for the facilitators to fill out a job selection form. Following the explanation of the Job Selection form, you will find instructions for the selection of facilitators.

The Job Selection Form allows the teacher to determine which Action Group the students will be in. It also helps the students recognize that some jobs in which they might be interested are part of a specific Action Group. While the students don't select specific jobs on this form, such as Press Secretary or Digital Coordinator, they can alert you that they are interested in a specific job within the Action Group. For instance, if several students are interested in the job of File Clerk, you can either assign one or have the students from the Documentation Group elect one. You could even appoint one as head File Clerk and have two assistants, if you like. You know your students best; this form allows you to make decisions on placement of students, but it also allows the students some input, some choice and voice, into what job responsibilities they choose to assume for the project. You will need to create job descriptions for any Topic-specific Action Groups that you choose to have so that the students know in advance what the general job responsibilities for that group(s) will be. Be sure to also write the name of any Topic-specific Action Group(s) on the blank space on the Job Selection form.

Make sure each student realizes that he or she can be in only one Action Group but will also be in a Research Group in addition to the Action Group. Students may take on additional jobs as long as they are part of the appropriate Action Group. The Press Secretary should be a member of the Media Group and the File Clerk, Journalist, Digital Coordinator and Scrapbook Coordinator should be a member of the Documentation Group. Because their jobs can be so time-consuming, the Journalist, Digital Coordinator, File Clerk, and Scrapbook Coordinator should not be a chairperson or co-chairperson of his or her Action Group.

The Job Selection form prompts students to rank their job preferences by instructing them to place a 1 in the blank beside the group you want to be in the most and a 2 in the blank beside your second choice. The students will be reminded to first review the job descriptions of each group and job before selecting their group preference. Facilitators (already elected by the group) cannot select any other jobs because their job is so demanding, and they must oversee all other jobs.

Selection of Facilitators

The selection of facilitators should be the responsibility of the entire class. The class must propose names of candidates and then vote by secret ballot. It is advisable that the election be preceded by a discussion of the role of the facilitators. Facilitators, it should be pointed out, help to orchestrate the entire project—they lead the Community-Action team into action! It should be stressed that this is not a popularity contest.

Each person nominated for the job of facilitator should be made aware of the responsibilities of the job and be willing to take on those responsibilities. It is a good idea for each of the nominees to prepare a three-minute speech. They can deliver it in front of the class before the election is held. The nominees should address the reasons that they think they should be selected as a facilitator.

Creating a Service-Learning Timeline

A timeline is simply a tool used to:

- Organize the service-learning experience (working timeline)
- Exhibit the chronological progression of the project (documentary timeline)

Working Timeline Creating a working timeline gives the students a choice and voice as to when different parts of the project should be completed. It helps them plan and organize their work. They should begin the working timeline after their initial research is completed and they have chosen the actual problem they are going to tackle, having decided upon the action(s) they will take. This timeline should deal with larger aspects of the project, using such rough headings as:

- Research completed
- Begin media contacts about project

- Begin final video (dubbing all project tapes)
- Begin final timeline to document project
- Have scrapbook completed
- Mail in grant application
- Start work on civic club presentations

This timeline is a working timeline, not a specific, neat timeline etched in stone. The students must deal with larger segments of time, such as months, for this outline. Actual dates are too specific for the working timeline. If it looks like a messy scratch piece of paper, they've got it!

Documentary Timeline More advanced service-learning experiences may require a final timeline that serves to document the project. A documentary timeline should include specific dates and events. It should be neat. The students should refer to team notes or journals to produce the documentary timeline. Computer programs are available that produce very professional-looking timelines.

T-shirts Anyone?

A team T-shirt can be a good way to unify the service-learning students as well as a great way to advertise the service-learning experience itself. The T-shirt can be worn on any service-learning outing or presentation to help promote the team's objectives and accomplishments. The design should be connected to the service-learning topic and/or the team's goals. The process for designing a project T-shirt follows:

- Inform the class members that they will have the opportunity to design a T-shirt that will be representative of their service-learning experience.
- As a whole-class activity or an activity carried out by the Public Relations Action Group, brainstorm ideas for the T-shirt for no more than five to ten minutes on an overhead of the Idea Jot Board.
- Divide the class into four or five groups. Each group should have pencils, crayons, or colored pencils and one T-shirt design form (see Appendix A).
- Each group should choose one of the ideas from the brainstormed list on the Jot Board, and then create a T-shirt design based on the chosen idea.
- Encourage the students to think about a design for both the front and back of the T-shirt.

- Display all the designs for a few days and then have the class vote on the design the class likes best.
- Decide on the color for the T-shirts and arrange to have the T-shirts printed using this design when you have the money to do so.

Communication Techniques

Service-learning has been found to improve communication skills in students. Does this mean students involved in service-learning will develop a gift for gab? No, that's not what it means. What it does mean is that through service-learning, students can develop better communication skills, skills that can benefit them both now and in the future. This section offers procedures, hints, and ideas designed to enhance communication skills as well as the service-learning project. Be sure to check the communication listing in Appendix A as some of the tips are included only in handout form.

Designing Action Stationery

It is fun and important for the students to take part in creating a design for the stationery that will be used for all correspondence related to the service-learning experience. The design should be connected to the service-learning topic and/or the team. This design can also be used as a logo on project flyers or posters. Using a consistent design on all service-learning materials helps to create an identity for the project among the students as well as in the community. Creating a stationery design can involve the following steps:

- Tell the class members that they are going to design the stationery layout that will be used for all of their letters and notes concerning the service-learning experience.
- As a whole-class activity or an activity carried out by the Public Relations Action Group, brainstorm ideas for the stationery on an overhead of the Idea Jot Board.
- Divide the class into four or five groups. Each group should have pencils and one Action Stationery design form (see Appendix A).
- Each group should choose one of the ideas from the brainstormed list on the jot board. The groups should then formulate a stationery design based on the chosen idea.
- Display the designs and have the class vote on the design the class likes best.

- If possible, recreate the design using an advanced graphic design software package. If you have an artist in the class, you can use an original drawing. You can then use a scanner to import the original drawing into a computer.
- Make photocopies of the design or save the design digitally (on the computer) for future use.

Gaining Support for Your Service-Learning Project

Who?   You need the support of the community in general. Specifically, you need the support of the following people or groups:

- Your school principal
- Your system superintendent and board of education
- Your local elected officials, such as the mayor, city council members, or the board of commissioners
- Community organizations, agencies, and businesses that might have an interest in the community need and/or be a potential community partner
- Your local newspapers and other media representatives

When?   The early bird gets the worm! The earlier you establish support the better! Inform your principal early and regularly about the project. Ask for his or her guidance from time to time. Invite the principal, the system superintendent, the board of education, and your community partners to any press conferences you hold. Send the local media press releases regularly, especially during a special event, such as when you schedule a community workday, guest speaker, or a field trip.

How?   One, by mail, two by email, three by phone! If your school system has an interoffice mailing system, you can easily, at no expense, send letters to the school officials. You can take any press releases to the newspaper offices, or you can email them. Calling on the telephone is a nice way to remind people about your project and to follow up on any written correspondence the group sends.

Conducting Action Surveys

A survey is simply a tool used to:

- Determine public opinion (opinion survey)
- Determine specific information through analysis and observation (observation/information survey)

Opinion Survey Some service-learning experiences may require that the students determine the opinions of others. For instance, they might want to find out how other students feel about the cafeteria food or whether drugs are a problem in their community. Where do they start? They cannot just make a statement about how people feel—they must investigate to find out exactly how they feel (see the Let's Talk handout in Appendix A). They can easily do this by conducting an opinion survey. In developing an opinion survey, they should create a list of questions to ask. You should advise them not to ask more than ten questions—preferably, no more than six.

The students can ask the questions aloud to each person and record the responses on a tally sheet if the responses are likely to be simple, such as yes or no. If the answers will require more than a simple response, the students can create a survey with enough space after each question. They can then distribute the survey to people to fill out and return to the student at a later time.

After the survey responses are completed, the students can tabulate the results. The more people surveyed, the more valid the results. A brief word of advice—if the students are going to hand out the survey to respondents, be sure that it is neat and easy to read. It is always better, of course, if the survey is typed or computer generated. Opinion surveys can be effective in determining the significance of issues as well as ultimately generating support for your ideas. Be sure to have the students thank the participants for their help!

Observation/Information Survey Service-learning students may need to conduct observation or information surveys in order to verify the need for the proposed project or to help established organizations gather information and statistics.

As two students measured the base of the monument, another student carefully recorded the measurements in the group's Research Plan Book. The HARD ROCK Kids service-learning group were conducting an observation/information survey for the SOS! (Save Outdoor Sculptures) program to document information about the local monuments. They had to determine the exact size, the material, the inscriptions, the condition, and other such things concerning their assigned monuments. This information was entered into the Smithsonian database for documentation of monuments in the United States.

An observation/information survey may also require additional research, as the SOS! surveys did. The students had to research the history of the monuments. This task required many trips to the library, sifting through old newspapers—some over ninety years old—and conducting many interviews. One student even had to make a trip to the cemetery to determine a sculptor's exact name and date of death.

Presenting the Action

Once the students are far enough along in their service-learning experience that they can see some results, they must think about presenting what they have achieved to the community. A presentation may even be required if they are asking for approval of some aspect of the service-learning experience or if the students are requesting funding for some part of it. The Meeting Tips handout, in Appendix A, should be helpful in making sure that the students know how to conduct a presentation and how to behave during one.

- Be sure to arrange a time for the students to have a class discussion about what might be presented or addressed at the meeting or the forum the students plan to attend. Some of the students can play the parts of the committee or council members; some can play the parts of the students at the meeting. Make sure that all points of view are represented in the sociodrama. You may want to give the students a copy of the Role-playing the Action handout in Appendix A. Allow about five minutes for the students to role-play. This can be helpful in preparing the students for the real thing.

- Audiovisuals, such as videos, charts, or slideshows, are very effective for presentations. If you are specifically asking a club or organization for something, whether it is money or some other type of support, it is very helpful to state this. Each member of the organization should be given this request in the form of a handout.

- The students, not the teacher, should deliver the presentations, although the teacher should be present, if possible, at the presentations. Alternating the presenters at different presentations is also to be encouraged because it gives more students the opportunity to do a presentation.

Preparing for a Press Conference

1. Step 1: Notify the Press.

   The Media Action Group will need to contact the newspapers and all the radio and television stations in your area informing them that your class will be holding a press conference—a meeting to inform the public of an important occurrence—and that you would like for them to be present. Be sure to include the *place*, the *time*, and the *circumstances* for the press conference.

2. Step 2: Prepare for a Press Conference.

   - The Media Action Group will prepare a *press release*. Make enough copies for each invited newspaper and anyone else whom you have invited, such as government officials, school personnel, and/ or civic organization representatives.

- Prepare the meeting place for effective communication and the comfort of the guests. If it is to be held in your classroom, you might want to create an effective atmosphere in your room by rearranging furniture, setting up a podium, having a welcome banner over the door, and arranging for refreshments for the visitors.

- Create a "Press Conference" banner to place above your room door. You can also create colorful signs directing people to the press conference.

- Each member of the group should be dressed neatly and should be prepared for the event by a brief run-through of the press conference (dress rehearsal).

- Set up greeters to meet each of the invited guests and escort them to the press conference. The individual greeter should see to the concerns of the person he or she is greeting, such as introductions and seating arrangements.

- Upon entering the press conference, each invited guest should be directed to a seat and handed a copy of the press release.

- When all guests have been properly introduced and seated, the Press Secretary will take the podium and again thank the guests for coming. Then he or she will proceed to read the press release. At the conclusion of the reading, the Press Secretary will then take any questions from the press.

- The press conference should not take long—maybe ten or fifteen minutes, unless you serve refreshments. Please refer to the Press Conference handout in Appendix A.

Assessment Tools and Techniques

The primary purpose of assessment is to inform educators, students, and parents about the degree of understanding and ability of the students in relation to the objectives of the instruction. Assessment instruments are tools for collecting data about the levels of student understanding. Types of assessment can and should include more than pencil-and-paper tests. In the classroom, assessment tools can include projects, portfolios, reflections, quizzes, homework, and presentations as well as traditional tests.

We know service-learning can be both rewarding and exciting for students. As a teacher, however, how can you assess the learning that takes place? In this time of accountability in education, it is essential to justify the time spent on any activity including service-learning activities. Although traditional assessments such as quizzes and tests can be useful in assessing student learning, they may not be as effective as other types of assessment for evaluating service-learning activities. This section includes procedures and ideas for assessment as well as some tools for assessing service-learning. They are by no means the only forms of assessment that can be used in service-learning. The handouts in Appendix A include forms for tracking service hours, weekly reports, and student self-evaluation as well as rubrics for assessing the level of reflection.

Charting Your STARS

Star charting is a method used to celebrate and reward excellent performance as well as to motivate those students who need to be motivated. Materials needed include poster board, a marker, the student list, a calendar, and stick-on stars. To make a star chart, use the following steps:

1. On the poster board, print each student's name, one below the other.
2. Create a chart for each month of the project with a column drawn for each project day.
3. Place a column labeled *Total* at the end of each month. Stars are earned both individually and as a group.

Examples of how the stars can be earned follow:

- Upon completion of the plans for each week—for actions planned and actions taken
- Upon completion of actions, whether it is a press release sent, a community resource contacted, or a reflective activity completed
- For exceptional behavior
- For work done outside the class
- For meetings attended, such as city council and board of education meetings
- Upon completion of research—more than one star can be given for bigger bites of the project; for instance, you can offer ten or more stars for completion of long-term assignments

Suggestions for Using a Star Chart At the beginning of the time period, whether it is monthly, six weeks, or nine weeks, designate the number of stars each student needs to earn for a reward. Make the goal high enough to motivate them but not so high that it is unattainable by most of the students. Awarding one star per day for on-task behavior is a good idea; essentially the students earn a star automatically unless it is pulled for behavior problems or off-task behavior. In addition to this star, others can, of course, be earned for achievements during the day.

Star Reward System Students who have earned the preset number of stars for that time period can participate in an Action Reward Activity, celebrating their outstanding performance. The following are suggestions for Action Rewards:

- Pizza party in class (students can pay)
- Ice cream party in class or at a local ice cream parlor within walking distance, if at all possible
- Movie during class with snacks
- Skating party on a Saturday
- A special prize for the student with the most stars

Using the Action Self-Evaluation Form

The use of the Action Self-Evaluation form (see Appendix A) is not mandatory for a successful service-learning experience, but it is an effective way to get the students to take responsibility for their own actions and learn to evaluate themselves accurately. In combination with the Weekly Action Report form (see Appendix A), it is also an effective way for you to assess the work done and determine a final grade for the students. Self-evaluation is used to help the students reflect on their performance and to motivate them to greater action.

Directions for using the Action Self-Evaluation form follow:

- Toward the end of each school-reporting period, hand out a copy of the Action Self-Evaluation form to each of the students.
- Discuss the five areas listed on the instrument and what each means.
- Go over the directions at the top of the page with them.
- Explain that they should add their score on those five areas (with 1 being the lowest and 10 being the highest) and double the total to get *their* grade.
- Inform them that *you* will also determine a grade for each of them based on this instrument.
- If their score is within ten points of your score and theirs is higher, then they can keep their score or grade.

- If they have evaluated themselves *more than* ten points higher than you have, then they get *your* score or grade.
- If they have evaluated themselves lower than you have, then they will keep *their* score or grade.

Weekly Action Report

The Weekly Action Report can serve as an evaluation instrument as well as a method for the entire class to learn of the activities and accomplishments of those in other Action Groups and those with separate jobs during each week of the project. Individual students as well as those working on a group project can use the Weekly Action Report form located in Appendix A.

Directions for using the Weekly Action Report follow:

- Plan a time for sharing what each student or group has accomplished each week.
- Give a copy of the Weekly Action Report form to each student or group to fill out. This should take about ten minutes.
- Have each student or one member of a group read or relate a summary of the weekly activities and accomplishments from the Weekly Action Report form.
- For those students working in Action Groups, each week the job of the reporter should alternate so that each person in each Action Group will have the opportunity to share with the class.

Assessing Reflection

Reflection is the process of looking back on actions taken to determine what has been gained, lost, or achieved and connecting those conclusions to future actions and societal contexts. In service-learning, reflection refers to the creative and critical thinking processes that are responsible for converting the service-learning experience into a productive learning experience (Kinsley and McPherson 1995). Assessing a student's reflective writings is an effective way to determine the level of learning that has taken place.

James Bradley (1995) categorized three levels of reflection that can be used when assessing the level of student learning in service-learning. Bradley's levels of reflection are:

- Level One: Observation (recognition of a dilemma)
- Level Two: Analysis (responding, framing, and reframing)
- Level Three: Synthesis (experimentation and strategy selection)

Bradley's (1995) three levels have been connected to the three levels of the Developmental Service-Learning Typology, thus providing a developmental framework for assessing reflection. Bradley's Level One, Observation, corresponds to the typology's Community-Service level and the lower stage of the Community-Exploration level. Bradley's Level Two, Analysis, corresponds to the highest stage of the Community-Exploration level. His Level Three, Synthesis, corresponds to the Community-Action level. (Note: for students providing service at the Community-Action level but still operating on a concrete operational level of cognition, only the reflective levels of Observation and Analysis would apply and are incorporated into the typology.) (See chart in Appendix B.)

You will find rubrics in Appendix A with criteria that relate to each of the Observation, Analysis, and Synthesis levels as well as fourth rubric designed for students operating at lower cognitive levels. These rubrics can be used to help understand and implement a service-learning experience as well as determine the level of the reflection. Please also refer to the suggested reflective activities in Chapters 2, 3, and 4. Each of the activities listed is designed to be appropriate for students working at the related level of service-learning and can be assessed using the rubrics in Appendix A.

Adapting the Reflective Activities

You may want to adapt and extend the basic reflective activities listed in Chapters 2, 3, and 4 by providing the students with questions that help them think more deeply and critically about the service experience. Make sure that you connect the activity directly to the service experience and allow for different styles of learning. If you are going to guide the reflection, be sure to pick an activity that is appropriate to both the developmental and service-learning level of the students involved. Choosing at least one question from each of the following three categories helps to balance the reflection.

What Happened?

- What did you observe?
- What service did you provide?
- How did you feel about what you did?
- What concern/problem was addressed?
- What were the results of your project?
- What was noteworthy about the service experience?

What Difference Did It Make?

- What new skill did you learn?
- Did the service experience help you identify a new area of interest?
- How was the experience different from what you expected?
- How did the service experience impact the way you view the problem area? The community? Yourself?
- What did you learn about the service recipient and/or the community?
- How did the community benefit from the service project?

What Are the Broader Implications?

- Did you help overcome the community challenge? How?
- Will any type of action need to be taken in the future? Why?
- What contributes to the success or downfall of a service-learning experience like this?
- What learning occurred that can be applied to other areas?
- What advice would you share with future service providers?
- What would you like to learn more about because of this service-learning experience?

References

Bradley, James. 1995. "A Model for Evaluating Student Learning in Academically Based Service." In *Connecting Cognition and Action: Evaluation of Student Performance in Service Learning Courses,* edited by M. Troppe, 13–26. Providence, RI: Campus Compact.

Brown, John Seely, Allan Collins, and Paul Duguid. 1989. "Situated Cognition and the Culture of Learning." *Educational Researcher* 18 (1): 32–42.

"Franklin Co. 'Green Gang' Kids Talk Trash and Save Their County Money." 1993. *Athens Daily News,* March 8, 3.

Kinsley, Carol W., and Kate McPherson. 1995. *Enriching the Curriculum Through Service Learning.* Alexandria, VA: Association for Supervision and Curriculum Development.

McCarthy, Rebecca. 1993. "Kids Talk Trash, and It Saves the County Money." *The Atlanta Journal/The Atlanta Constitution,* March 7, D1.

National Council for the Social Studies. About NCSS [cited September 10 2006]. Available from http://www.ncss.org/about/.

Osborn, Alex. 1963. *Creative Imagination.* 3rd ed. New York: Charles Scribner.

Parnes, Sidney. 1967. *Creative Behavior Guidebook*. New York: Charles Scribner.

Schine, Joan, ed. 1997. *Service Learning*. Chicago: The University of Chicago,

"Students Have Ideas for Landfill." 1991. *The NEWS Leader*, March 7, 13.

Terry, Alice W. 2000. "An Early Glimpse: Service Learning from an Adolescent Perspective." *The Journal of Secondary Gifted Education* 11 (3): 115–34.

Tomlinson, Carol Ann. 1999. *Differentiated Classroom: Responding to the Needs of All Learners*. Alexandria, VA: Association for Supervision and Curriculum Development.

Torrance, E. Paul. 1995. *Why Fly?* Norwood, NJ: Ablex Publishing Corporation.

"Way to Go!" 1994. *Teen*, 128–31.

Wheeler, Adrienne. 1994. *The Donahue Show*. New York: National Broadcasting Company, July 22.

Chapter Six

Incorporating Service-Learning into the School and Community

Service-learning initiatives usually begin with an eager teacher—or group of school and community members—who have attended a service-learning conference, visited a service-learning site, or otherwise been exposed to the excitement that surrounds service-learning. Filled with enthusiasm for what they have seen, they are often anxious to become involved in engaging the youth in their school or community in this phenomenon. But where should one start? Is service-learning appropriate only in a traditional classroom setting? Can service-learning be integrated successfully into other aspects of the school or in a community-based setting as well?

Young people are usually introduced to the ethic of service through a family commitment to volunteering or through community service activities organized by their places of worship, schools, or youth-serving and leadership organizations such as 4-H Clubs, Girl Scouts and Boy Scouts, Boys and Girls Clubs, Key Club and Builders Club, and National Honor Society. The type of service usually encouraged by these groups is simple volunteerism, although some groups are advancing higher-level service experiences such as the optional Gold Award Projects sponsored by the Girl Scouts. Volunteerism can certainly play a role in helping youth develop a sense of self and community; however, more gains would be possible if these social institutions supported and fostered service-learning. Picking up discarded aluminum cans from a stream bank or the side of a road on Earth Day is service. If the students return to the organization after a day of service and reflect on the reasons their community is littered with empty cans and then develop and implement an action plan designed to address the problem, such as creating a recycling plan or advocating for a bottle bill, they are engaged in service-learning. This chapter will look at why and how service-learning can be incorporated into school- and community-based settings.

Incorporating Service-Learning into Schools

Service-Learning in Middle Schools Through Curriculum Integration

What should be the curriculum for young adolescents? The National Middle School Association in its position paper calls for curriculum in middle schools that is planned in units that last several weeks, using complex tasks and essential questions rather than day-to-day lessons. It states that units should be organized around a theme or integrated by a melding of teacher goals and students' questions rather than through a separate subject format more appropriate for high-school students (National Middle School Association 2003).

In exemplary middle schools, while academic standards are organized by discipline, concepts and essential questions that function both within and across disciplines should also be incorporated. Broad concepts that cut across disciplines provide the basis of an integrated curriculum design. In designing integrated units in middle schools, teachers on teams that represent different disciplines examine the standards, key concepts, and essential questions of their particular discipline. Then they bring their discipline-based priorities to the team to discover overlaps in the concepts that undergird each discipline. From this exercise, teams develop integrated units that can be of varying lengths, from several weeks to months. For example, the concept of *systems* could be the basis of an effective integrated unit. Systems are central to social studies through social systems in society; to science through systems in the body or nature; to language arts through systems of language, literature, and reading; and to math through operating systems and systems of measurement.

Two dimensions of an integrated curriculum are (1) curriculum concepts that emerge from the intersection of personal and social concerns and (2) the higher-order skills that students need in order to explore such curriculum concepts. A third dimension involves broad and enduring concepts that should permeate the content of any curriculum, particularly if one of the goals is to have a lasting and influential impact on the lives of students. Democracy, human dignity, and cultural diversity are broad and enduring concepts that make up the third dimension (Muth and Alvermann 1998).

Service-learning fits well into all three dimensions of an integrated curriculum. For instance, a concept like *systems*, mentioned earlier, can be effective as the basis for an integrated unit that includes service-learning. In one service-learning experience (see SWaMP Kids, Chapter 5), the students became interested in developing a recycling program in their school. This evolved over three years into the seventh graders writing a 750-page state-required Solid Waste Management Plan for their county. Following the concept of *systems* in social studies, these students discovered firsthand about systems in society. How does government work? Because this service-learning experience involved issues important to county government and to democracy in general, they had to learn how the county government operated and, in essence, how democracy works. They also attended and presented at meetings of the county officials. Because they had to use both oral and written communication skills throughout the project, they had to effectively incorporate *systems* of language. They also had to read and interpret high-level material on waste management, utilizing *systems* of reading comprehension. Because their project involved issues of environmental concern, they had to learn about *systems* involving the environment. How do landfills affect the ecological system? These students also had to incorporate math *systems* using basic math system skills to determine the amount of waste that was disposed of over a year in five cities. They also had to use more advanced prediction and estimation skills to determine how to achieve a 25 percent reduction of the waste stream over a ten-year period.

Other ideas conducive for the incorporation of service-learning into integrated units are transition, interdependence, structures, resolution, growth, change, and choices.

Incorporating Service-Learning in Small Learning Communities for High Schools

Many educators now believe that smaller, more closely knit schools are safer schools that can narrow the gap in achievement between middle-class, white students and poor, minority students. In recent years, both public and private funding has been made available to schools, especially high schools in urban environments that have serious problems concerning student attendance, discipline, violence, achievement scores, and dropout rates, to reorganize and subdivide their large comprehensive schools into autonomous small learning communities (SLCs). As part of the small schools movement, freshmen, and in some cases eighth graders, often enter Success Academies that are designed to ease the transition from middle school to high school. The Success Academies help low-achieving students stay in school by offering a supportive environment that enables them to achieve academically while exploring their interests. These students are then better prepared to choose the type of SLCs they want to attend in their final years of high school.

There is no one model for the creation of small learning communities; however, most have a thematic or career focus and flexible scheduling, and feature a collaborative, relevant, student-centered curriculum that is connected to the world outside of school. Students and their parents jointly select a particular SLC based on the curricular theme, career focus of the school, or particular instructional focus. Because the class groupings are small and the teachers and students stay together for multiple years, individual members of the learning community know each other well. This promotes a sense of belonging and allows teachers to adapt instruction to the students' particular strengths and needs, which in turn helps to motivate the students to explore topic-related questions and create products demonstrating their knowledge.

Community involvement and community partnerships are featured in many SLC models. Teachers are encouraged to work with community partners to design curricula grounded in work-based learning experiences and service opportunities. Because service-learning and SLCs share so many common threads, service-learning could be easily woven into the fabric of SLCs. It is hoped that professional development seminars for SLC teachers will include sessions on facilitating service-learning. Service-learning could then be incorporated into the SLC curriculum to provide the structure for teachers to extend the instructional material into community contexts and involve the students in active, authentic inquiry. By using service-learning as the delivery system for the kind of real-world, engaging learning experience desired by SLCs, students could expand their learning experience to include either curriculum-related service-learning experiences or service-learning internships that introduce the youth to workplace situations.

Character Education

Character education has come into its own in recent years. The primary focus of any character-education program is to help students develop knowledge and life skills in order to enhance ethical and responsible behavior. Embedded in character education are guidelines for successful living. Respect and responsibility are at the core of its directive for youth. Although there is not a singular way for providing character education, basic principles do exist. Eleven principles have been identified for schools to use in developing a character-education program. One principle for the development of character is giving students opportunities for moral action. Because students learn best by doing, they need opportunities to apply values such as responsibility and fairness in everyday interactions and discussions. Service-learning is an effective way for students to develop a practical understanding of the requirement of fairness, cooperation, and respect while at the same time practicing moral skills and behavioral habits of being good citizens (Likona 1996).

Service-Learning with Students with Learning Disabilities

Service-learning can provide students with disabilities the ideal context to both acquire and maintain new skills. Placing these students in service roles through service-learning experiences gives them valuable opportunities to give back as well as to connect with their community. Through service-learning opportunities, these students learn and practice functional skills in actual environments, environments like the ones they will be in when they are no longer in school. This is important in helping students with learning disabilities get a head start at gaining skills they will need in the future.

Unfortunately, some special education teachers have expressed that many do not perceive what their students do in the community as service-learning because the learning is not at a high level. Referencing the Developmental Service-Learning Typology, it is clear that students with learning disabilities can participate in service-learning at the appropriate level for their abilities. Community-Service service-learning is certainly appropriate for students with learning disabilities, although some learning-disabled students, of course, may be capable of reaching higher levels of service-learning than others. In reflecting on their service-learning experience at the Community-Service level, these students will describe what happened and the people who were involved during the service-learning experience. They will also share parts of the experience that were meaningful and share their feelings about the entire experience. To assess what students working at this level have gained from their experience, it is suggested that teachers use the Preliminary Reflection Rubric for Community-Service service-learning. Teachers working with learning-disabled students who function at a higher level of cognition should read through the rubrics and select whichever rubric is most appropriate for the students' level of cognition (see Appendix A).

Gifted Education

For gifted students, schools need not only to design and implement learning opportunities within the classroom but also to identify learning resources and opportunities in the community that are integrated with those of the classroom. Unfortunately, schools seldom provide gifted students with opportunities beyond the classroom. In general, our schools have not effectively provided appropriate challenges for the gifted. Far too often, curricula for the gifted is organized by subjects, even though most real problems involve interdisciplinary study (Passow 1989).

Community-Action service-learning offers strong affective and process components that complement cognitive components and is effective in sensitizing gifted students to community problems and needs while incorporating interdisciplinary study. One of these components, problem solving, is important in developing cognition in gifted students. The types of cognitively demanding tasks that we encounter in the day-to-day world are different from those we encounter in the classroom. Problems studied in the classroom are typically well defined, with all the information needed to solve them being provided. The issue of transference is called into question when these skills are taught in isolation and then applied to real-world problems, and we cannot assume that transfer will occur spontaneously. Problems in the real world are more likely to be ill defined, to be lacking in required information, and, in many cases, not to have a known correct solution (Nickerson 1994). What service-learning does is put problem solving to work in the real world for gifted youth, thereby enhancing the chance that transference will occur in other future real-world situations.

Not only does Community-Action service-learning have the capability of helping the gifted reach their cognitive, affective, and creative potential as they seek solutions to society's ever-increasing challenges, it also has been shown to be an effective, differentiated curriculum for instruction with the gifted. Ernest Boyer expressed the power of service-learning to cognitive and moral development when he stated, "Knowledge unguided by an ethical compass is potentially more dangerous than ignorance itself" (Boyer 1995, 179). Through their participation in Community-Action service-learning, gifted students learn to use their gifts in socially constructive ways, which fosters the development of an ethical compass.

Incorporating Service-Learning into the Community

Community Organizations and Faith-based Initiatives

While implementing service-learning in a school-based setting is probably the most common approach, service-learning has also been implemented effectively by community-based youth-serving organizations and faith-based initiatives as an after-school or summer activity. One of the authors has worked as a service-learning consultant with a number of successful, non-traditional service-learning experiences undertaken by inner-city, at-risk youth and has found that the power of service-learning to engage and empower at-risk youth is an exciting transformation to watch. Strangely, youth with lower academic achievement, especially those from lower socioeconomic backgrounds, are much less likely to be offered opportunities to become engaged in school-based service-learning, even though they could benefit enormously from exposure to new ideas and role models as well as the opportunity to develop and exercise their own choice and voice. With the inclusion of community-based organizations and faith-based initiatives in the Corporation for National and Community Service's Learn and Serve America grant programs, it is hoped that more community-based and faith-based organizations will offer quality service-learning experiences to at-risk youth and fill this void. Depending on the type of sponsoring organization, a curriculum connection may not be specifically emphasized in community-based service-learning, but real-world and academic learning is often apparent as evidenced in the following examples.

Bill of Rights for Children in Care Project   Six teenage girls taught and housed at a foster care group home undertook the Bill of Rights for Children in Care service-learning project in 1992. The girls had undergone many new experiences during the previous year, culminating in a decision to participate in the Community Problem Solving program and create a service-learning project that would enable youth in foster care to receive the same rights as other children.

The girls were unable to be placed in individual foster homes because of their past histories. For the most part, their instinctive abilities had helped them survive their unfortunate circumstances, however, as they entered their mid-teens some were beginning to flounder. Fortunately, in 1991, the girls were offered the opportunity to learn creative problem solving techniques under the auspices of a federal grant for at-risk children. The experience equipped the girls with the skills to address the many real-life challenges that they faced as well as the ability to harness their energies in a positive manner. As part of the grant, the girls participated in an academic problem solving competition and did so well in preliminary evaluations that they were invited to participate in the 1992 international problem solving competition hosted by the Future Problem Solving Program (FPSP). Their entry fees, housing, and food were paid for through the grant, but there were many things that the girls needed, including permission from the state to let them, as wards of the state, go to an out-of-state competition where they would be mixing with *"regular* kids" on a college campus. The girls also needed basic supplies such as toiletries, clothes, and suitcases. Using their newly honed problem solving skills, the teens overcame all these obstacles and went to the competition. They didn't place in the international problem solving competition, but they performed admirably well. Their greatest growth experience came from their fellowship with the other students at the competition, especially those involved in the Community Problem Solving program, the service-learning component of FPSP. The girls realized that many things that the *regular* teens at the competition took for granted were denied to youth in foster care, such as the ability to get a driver's license, have regular contact with their siblings, be able to file a grievance and expect a response, or even attend religious services of their choice.

When they returned to the group home, the girls discussed their experience and decided that they needed to put their problem solving abilities to good use and create a real-life plan of action that would make a difference for children in care throughout the state. They organized a fellowship of teenagers in foster care, and surveyed the other foster care youth about the issues that most concerned them. After researching the issues, they worked together with other foster youth and their community partners to create and carefully word a Bill of Rights for Children in Care designed to improve the most pressing issues. The girls, who previously had a hard time making eye contact with adults, became very able speakers who were clearly passionate about their cause. During the next few months, they reported their findings and introduced their Bill of Rights for Children in Care to many civic groups and government agencies. These tenth and eleventh graders trained foster care workers at three different agencies on the issues facing foster children and how to be sensitive to those issues. They contacted local and state legislators, celebrities, and business people garnering support for the Bill of Rights.

Representatives from the group were appointed to the board of various youth-serving agencies as voting members, including the Governor's Commission on Children and Youth. In March of 1993, the group was presented with an official Proclamation from the state legislature honoring their work in developing the Bill of Rights for Children in Care. They were invited to take part in the 1993 Future Problem Solving International Conference, this time to participate in the Community Problem Solving competition. The girls presented their Bill of Rights for Children in Care project to hundreds of interested students and teachers from around the world and accepted the FPSP Director's Award for their outstanding work. Quite remarkable achievements for a group of girls that society had almost given up on!

Teen Pregnancy Project The Emerald Youth Foundation (EYF) is a faith-based community organization that serves inner-city children and youth at multiple sites within a federally designated empowerment zone in Knoxville, Tennessee. EYF enhances the spiritual, academic, personal, physical, and social skills of youth through a structured youth-development program, which includes an after-school and summer setting. Originally started by the Emerald Avenue United Methodist Church as a way to reach out to its community, it has evolved into a prototype for effective youth-serving organizations. The youth at each center participate in elementary-, middle-, or high-school groups. EYF emphasizes spiritual, academic, recreational, enrichment, and relational activities and has its own training facility for staff, AmeriCorps members, and volunteers—Emerald University. The adults leading service-learning with the youth are trained in facilitating service-learning and use the service-learning materials created by the authors and incorporated into the Emerald University curriculum.

The EYF youth participate in service-learning activities one afternoon a week, with projects normally lasting for six weeks. The students brainstorm concerns in their community, select an underlying challenge, and create an action plan. They organize themselves into self-selected Action Groups, with each group carrying out a specific piece of the action plan. They learn responsibility for themselves and others.

The EYF young people have implemented many exciting community service-learning activities. A teen pregnancy service-learning experience undertaken in 2003 by a middle-level EYF group stands out as one that challenged both the young people and their leader. Even after the youth had brainstormed significant concerns in their community and selected teen pregnancy as the focus for their service-learning experience, the team members couldn't reach a consensus that teen pregnancy was all that bad. During the class discussion, comments such as "having a baby at least gives you someone to love who loves you back" or that teen pregnancy "improved the life of my cousin who got off drugs once she became pregnant" were heard. After other similar issues were brought up, the leader knew that this project wouldn't be as clear-cut as the GraffitiBusters project had been the previous year.

After the group researched statistics about teen pregnancy and interviewed community members, it decided that this was indeed a big problem in their community—one they wanted to help solve. Because of the nature of their project, they had to overcome several obstacles. For instance, some of the more obvious solutions for reducing teen pregnancy, such as the distribution of condoms, weren't viable actions for middle-school students at a faith-based organization. The group decided to use a two-pronged approach:

- Create an awareness program designed to reduce teen pregnancy
- Collect baby supplies for girls who were already pregnant and living at a local home for unwed mothers

The group was successful in both phases of their service-learning experience. They spoke passionately to community groups and other youth about the problem, and one youth won the annual slogan contest sponsored by the local health department. As part of their campaign to reduce teen pregnancy through awareness and abstinence, the team created two brochures, one for teens and one for parents. The following poem written by Stephanie, an eighth-grader who was one of the girls who initially saw some benefits to teen pregnancy, was included in both brochures:

> **A** girl loves a boy.
> The boy says I love you, too.
> **B**ut when it comes down to it
> You know what he wants to do.
> **S**TD's are what you can get or
> Maybe even a baby with a birth defect.
> **E**nd your teen years with a baby or two
> And see what you got yourself into.
> **N**o one understands, is what you may say
> And really you're the one who don't
> understand anywayz [sic]
> **T**ry to stay clean, try to stay away
> It's *abstinence* the only good way.

The bold letters in the poem spell out the word *absent*. As Stephanie explained her intent to her youth leader, "If you don't practice abstinence and get pregnant, you can pretty well count on the guy to be *absent*." This shift in thinking and values was brought about because of her participation in the service-learning experience. Perhaps becoming engaged in a service-learning experience like this and having something constructive to do with her time that also had a positive impact on the lives of others helped to make abstinence an even easier choice for her.

Leadership Organizations

Service-learning has the potential to provide a framework for richer and deeper service opportunities for youth leadership organizations that already promote individual or group service activities for youth. Service activities are often required by youth leadership organizations in order for their members to advance to a higher level within the organization, such as the Boy Scout service projects required to advance to the rank of Eagle Scout or Key Club members who are required to fulfill fifty hours of service per year. The mission of Key Club International is *to provide service, build character, and develop leadership*. Each student-led high-school club has the option to select its own service project based on a local community need, or its members may participate in a Service/Major Emphasis Program suggested by Key Club International. Its Read and Lead initiative encourages high-school students to read to a young child at least one hour a week in order to encourage budding readers to learn to love books. Key Clubbers well versed in service-learning could use their service-learning skills to expand the basic Read and Lead program to fit the specific needs of the emergent readers in their community, or they could choose to develop an entirely different plan designed to address another community concern identified by the club members. Involvement in more comprehensive service projects grounded in service-learning might indeed enhance the leadership skills, citizenship, and character building that youth leadership organizations seek to develop.

Sustainability Issues

Some service-learning advocates are concerned that when a teacher who has effectively implemented service-learning in his or her classroom leaves a school due to retirement, transfer, or burnout, the service-learning program will cease to exist as a pedagogy in the school, no matter what the recognized benefits of service-learning are to the students, school, and community. In order for service-learning to be sustained in a school or school district, it needs to become an integral part of the school or district's organization and culture. Schools can implement a number of strategies in order for service-learning to be sustained. These strategies include making sure that service-learning is part of a shared vision of the school or district, incorporating service-learning activities into the curriculum, providing service-learning professional-development opportunities for faculty and administrators, establishing strong and supportive community partnerships, and continuously striving for improvement of the program (Fredericks 2002).

Ideally, service-learning should become a part of a shared vision for achieving academic goals and standards within the school so that decisions regarding spending, hiring, and planning are guided by that vision. Schools should also encourage shared leadership so that service-learning is not the domain of one person but something that is valued by leaders at many levels, including classroom teachers, administrators, students, parents, and community members. Shared vision and leadership usually leads to service-learning being considered a sound pedagogy that can engage youth more meaningfully in their education and included as a key component of curriculum development that is aligned with state standards. The school day must contain regular, structured time built in for curriculum planning and collaboration as well as time for professional development so that faculty and staff can deepen their understanding of service-learning. The school must also offer training and support services to community members so they learn the benefits to their organization or business of partnering with the school; begin to value youth as important community resources and contributors; and become strong supporters of service-learning and the school system. Finally, efforts should be made to continuously strengthen and improve service-learning experiences through school and community assessments that evaluate the basic program as well as changing curricula needs, student interests, and staff capacities.

Specific tactics that have proven to be helpful in some school systems for strengthening and sustaining service-learning programs include having service-learning specifically mentioned in the mission statement of the school or district, forming local service-learning advisory boards, developing strong community partnerships, and establishing service-learning requirements for graduation.

Mission Statements

Once the school or district has explored where service-learning fits within its mission, it should formally include service-learning in the wording of its mission statement. Service-learning should also become a strong component of the school improvement plan, strategic planning, policy development, and school reform initiatives. Service-learning advocates believe this inclusion to be crucial to sustaining service-learning should changes in leadership or cuts in funding occur.

Community Advisory Boards

It is often helpful for representatives from a cross section of the community to be identified and invited to serve on a school or community service-learning advisory board. Members can include teachers, youth, administrators, business leaders, and members of community organizations—anyone who can help communicate and support the benefits and goals of service-learning. After training in the fundamentals of service-learning, board members can help plan and develop goals, recruit community partners, perform community-needs assessments, showcase service-learning experiences publicly, and provide varying degrees of leadership that can assist in the implementation and advancement of service-learning. The roles and functions of each advisory board member should be spelled out clearly so that the group can operate cohesively.

Community Partnerships

Establishing effective community partnerships that involve elementary and secondary schools, higher education, community-based organizations, businesses, nonprofit organizations, and government agencies all working together to increase the resources, relationships, and community assets available for student learning and action is considered a key element of high-quality service-learning programs. The partnership approach necessitates a shift in viewing the service element of service-learning from one of students working on their own to provide service to the community to one of students working with and among community partners to assess needs and implement service. Creating effective service-learning partnerships is not an easy task and involves a long-term commitment by all partners in addition to the flexibility to adapt to the changing needs and perspectives of each partner as well as the community.

Developing community partners can be challenging for teachers due to the time constraints of their job. Unless they are fortunate enough to have an already-established community coalition or a service-learning liaison to assist them in locating resources, teachers often initially delegate the task of developing community partnerships to their students. The students are given opportunities during class time to identify a curriculum-related need area in the local community, after which they research and contact appropriate community organizations, agencies, and individuals for specific input or assistance. A simple service-learning project-specific partnership provides a limited, need-by-need view of the community. It is hoped, however, that these limited service-learning partnerships, partnerships that must be reinvented for each service-learning activity, will evolve into service-learning advisory boards and then, over time, into full-fledged, collaborative community partnerships capable of enhancing the capacity of all the partners to strengthen the community. It takes an enormous amount of time, knowledge, and wherewithal to plan, manage, and maintain effective service-learning community partnerships, but the benefits of ongoing districtwide partnerships are many. Besides the direct and indirect benefits to the community of coordinated, collaborative service projects, successful community partnerships play an important role in sustaining and institutionalizing service-learning.

Graduation Requirements

While more and more schools recognize the value of student service in the community and are requiring a specified number of service hours for graduation, the emphasis may be on volunteerism rather than service-learning. The good news is that the number of schools that are offering support to teachers interested in integrating service-learning into the curriculum is rising.

An exciting initiative that has the potential to embed quality service-learning in more high-school programs is graduation requirements that call for *culminating projects* from all seniors. Many of the desired outcomes of culminating projects are also outcomes associated with service-learning such as student-directed learning, youth engagement, in-depth investigation of issues, community involvement, service experiences that address an authentic need in the community, activities that have a measurable impact on the community, issues with a challenging focus, and opportunities for celebration, making service-learning a good fit with culminating projects. Because service-learning can be developmental and allows students to learn and apply knowledge in different ways, it provides an excellent strategy for enabling students at all levels of achievement to complete a culminating project.

References

Boyer, Ernest L. 1995. *The Basic School: A Community for Learning.* Princeton, NJ: Carnegie Endowment for the Advancement of Teaching.

Fredericks, Linda. 2002. "Learning that Lasts: How Service-Learning Can Become an Integral Part of Schools, States, and Communities." Education Commission of the States [cited September 20 2006]. Available from www.ecs.org/html/ProjectsPartners/nclc/NCLC_Publications.asp

Kluth, Paula. 2000. "Community-Referenced Learning and the Inclusive Classroom." *Remedial & Special Education* 21 (1): 19–27.

Likona, Thomas. 1996. "Eleven Principles of Effective Character Education." *Journal of Moral Education* 25 (1): 93–100.

Muth, K. Denise, and Donna E. Alvermann. 1998. *Teaching and Learning in the Middle Grades.* 2nd ed. Boston: Allyn & Bacon.

National Middle School Association. 2003. *This We Believe: Successful Schools for Young Adolescents.* Westerville, OH: National Middle School Association.

Nickerson, R. S. 1994. "The Teaching of Thinking and Problem Solving." In *Thinking and Problem Solving,* edited by R. J. Sternberg. San Diego: Academic Press.

Passow, A. Harry. 1989. "Educating Gifted Persons Who Are Caring and Concerned." *Gifted Education International* 6 (1): 5–7.

Appendix A

Reproducible Handouts and Transparency Masters

Idea Jot Board . . . Brainstorming Ideas

All group members should contribute ideas to be included on the **Jot Board**. Write down as many ideas as the group can think of by **jotting** them down on the **Jot Board**—even upside down or sideways. Simple phrases, words, symbols, or drawings are fine. All ideas, including *wild* and *crazy* ones, should be listed on the **Jot Board**.

CS, CE, CA

Abstract Shape

CS, CE, CA

The Community-Action Model

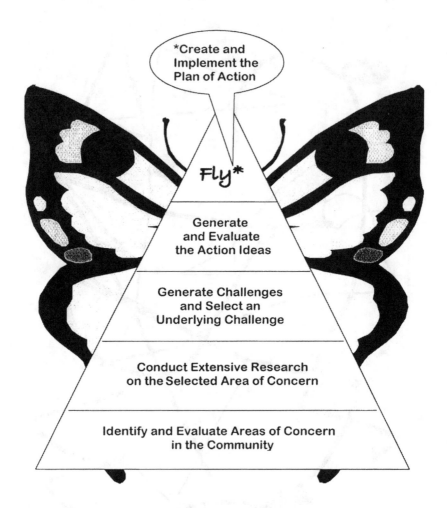

CA

Challenges Jot Board

All group members should identify as many problems or challenges to the situation as possible. Quickly jot down the ideas on the Jot Board—even upside down or sideways. All ideas, including *wild* and *crazy* ones, should be listed on the Jot Board. Circle the five or six that the team thinks present the biggest challenges.

CS, CE, CA

Action Ideas Jot Board

Place the Jot Board in the middle of the group. As a team, brainstorm as many different ways as possible to overcome the main challenge identified by your team. All ideas, including *wild* and *crazy* ones, should be listed on the Jot Board. Simple words, phrases, symbols, or drawings describing the Action Idea are fine. Narrow your brainstormed ideas by circling the six Action Ideas your team thinks are the most promising.

CE, CA

Action Ideas Evaluation Matrix

Place a phrase describing your top six Action Ideas on the numbered lines below. Select three of the phrases from the box of criteria examples (or create your own criteria) and list each on the grid. Weigh the benefits of each Action Idea individually by each criterion. Rank the six Action Ideas on a scale of 1 to 6—with the idea fitting the criterion the best getting a 6 and the one fitting it the least getting a 1.

Criteria Examples:
Which Action Idea will . . .

- be the most long-lasting?
- cost the least?
- be the most acceptable to ____?
- be the safest to do?
- be the most useful?
- be the quickest to implement?

1 = worst fit   6 = best fit

List your top SIX ideas below:

				Total
1.				
2.				
3.				
4.				
5.				
6.				

Add up the total for each Action Idea. Look at the Action Ideas with the higher scores. Think about whether any of these could be combined to create a more thorough plan. In the last column, put a check mark next to the two or three Action Ideas with the higher scores that would work well together to create an effective Action Plan.

CA

Facilitator's Group

Job Description

The job of Facilitator is, perhaps, the most important job of all. Each project usually has more than one Facilitator; it is suggested that two be assigned per class working on the service-learning project. Each Facilitator not only must be a leader but also must know what every other group is doing and act as a helper to these groups. You will be the extra *hands* and *voice* of the teacher. The hardest part of this job is that it separates you from your classmates. There is a difference between being a *leader* and being a *boss*. A *boss* commands, a boss demands, a boss is *bossy*. On the other hand, a *leader* motivates others toward a common goal. A *leader* respects others and, therefore, is respected by others. Facilitators are leaders. Be a leader, not a boss. Use your authority to give each group direction.

The teacher will monitor your facilitator notes and plans. Eventually you will monitor the plans of the other groups and sign your name after checking their plans each week. The teacher will, of course, give you direction and can intervene, if necessary. If you are uncomfortable with this responsibility, ask the teacher to let you *work into it* gradually. The Facilitators can divide this responsibility—check with your teacher about how to do this.

Each group will have its own job description. All job descriptions are listed in Appendix A of *Service-Learning . . . by Degrees*. Early on, you should become familiar with *all* job responsibilities for and within each group.

Although you will be helping to organize and coordinate the groups, you will also have varying responsibilities given to you by the teacher. These can range from helping to prepare presentations to doing additional research when needed. When a group *gets stuck*, you will need to try to find a way to get them *unstuck*. The teacher, of course, will be there to help, but you need to learn to handle some of the situations yourself. As a Facilitator, you have a *big* job and a lot of responsibility. Try to stay away from such words as *can't, impossible,* and *kids can't make a difference in the real world*. Help prove they can!

CA

Correspondence Action Group

Job Description

The Correspondence Action Group is responsible for making most of the community contacts. This includes writing and mailing letters, thank-you notes, press releases, and invitations; it also includes making many of the telephone contacts. You should have good *communication skills* to do this job well. This means that you should enjoy talking to people and be effective at expressing your ideas, both verbally and through writing.

You need to master the art of writing a business letter, preferably using a word-processing application on a computer. Address envelopes neatly and correctly. You need to work with the Public Relations Action Group to make sure your letters and packages are *decorated* nicely so that they come to the attention of and are opened by the correct person.

You will use the telephone in the school often, so you must learn to be very nice to the school secretary so that he or she will let you use the phone when needed. *Remember that tip!* Also, don't forget to say *thank you* and *please*!

You will need to keep an accurate, complete, and up-to-date list of all your contacts during the course of the Community-Action Project. All of these should be put into a binder or plan book.

Other groups will be giving you the ideas for letters that need to be written. However, it is up to you to express those ideas on paper effectively. Most letters should be neatly typed. Having written the letter, checked for spelling, and addressed the envelope (unless you are sending an email message), you should give it back to the group for review. Be sure to *save* it onto a computer disk, so if there are any changes that need to be made, you can make them easily. Make an extra copy for the files and give it to the File Clerk.

Remember to add *personality* to each letter. Use proper form and correct spelling, but don't forget to add that special quality that only a *kid* has—that real huggable quality of *childhood*. Let it ring through your letter or phone call so that your message will be received well and with a smile!

CA

Public Relations Action Group

Job Description

The job of the Public Relations Action Group, or PR, is a very crucial one. It includes many facets: art, advertising, slogans, and fundraising. Through effective public relations, you will get your message and your ideas out to the public. In other words, you are promoting not only your project but also yourselves. Being positive and creative is essential in this job. Having fun is a by-product of this job.

Not everyone in this group, but at least a couple, should be talented in art. You will be doing things from designing T-shirts to creating letterheads for your stationery and designing layouts for posters and flyers.

Though perhaps not as busy during the initial stages of the project, this group will become very busy during the final stages of the project when you will possibly be raising money and sending out information to the media. Although the Media Action Group will be responsible for the contacts, you will be working closely with this group in designing the material. Every letter that goes out to promote your group's project should be decorated on the outside with artwork and slogans, such as *Read me, Our project saves lives, Pick me, Kids can make a difference, Listen to the future*—anything clever that will make your letter stand out when it reaches its destination. This, of course, will be your job.

You will also be working closely with the Correspondence Action Group. Once your ideas for "selling yourselves" are achieved, many letters will need to be written. Once you compose the letter, the Correspondence Action Group can type and mail it or email it (sometimes, well-decorated envelopes sent through the mail receive much more attention than email requests).

Good public relations are essential if your project is to get any positive publicity. The more positive the publicity, the more effective the project will be.

CA

Media Action Group

Job Description

The Media Action Group plays a vital role during the service-learning project. From press releases to investigative work tracking possible media outlets, this job is a busy one. The members of this group should be creative, persistent, and able to write and communicate well. The Public Relations Action Group can help this group with ideas when needed; however, it is the ultimate responsibility of the Media Action Group to keep your project in the media.

Media is plural for medium. A medium, in the sense you will represent, is *a substance or agent through which anything acts or an effect is produced*. A newspaper is an advertising medium, as are magazines, radio, television, and the Internet.

Your group should research possible outlets for your *story*. Possibilities should be brainstormed as the project progresses. You, of course, should begin with your local newspaper. Send the local press personal press releases. Invite them to a *Press Conference* when you are doing something special. Have a prepared *Press Release*, and be sure to ask that they take a picture of the group. If your paper does not often take pictures, supply them with one. Have plenty of black-and-white photos of the group available to attach to the press releases.

As you get more involved in your project, you should increase your media contacts. Try for regional and state contacts after your local ones. What you hope for is that the Associated Press (AP) or the United Press International (UPI) will pick up your story and carry it in other newspapers and media throughout the United States. Contacting a *syndicated* writer from a larger newspaper can be beneficial. Syndicated writers publish their articles in as many as a hundred newspapers at once. You can contact the larger newspapers to determine who the syndicated writers are. Then read their columns to determine how to write your press release so that they might pick it up.

Don't forget how effective radio or television is. Contact your local and state stations first. National networks usually pick up from the state sources. You can, however, get the addresses of topical television shows such as *Oprah, 60 Minutes,* or *Dateline* and send them a one-page letter describing your project. You need to include articles about your project from newspapers with the letter. Using a copy of *TV Guide Magazine* can help you with your brainstorming. You will need to watch these TV shows or check the appropriate websites in order to get the addresses.

You should create a *Media Packet* to be sent on to your state and national media contacts. With the help of the Public Relations Action

Group, you can design a cover page for the information packet that includes the name of your Community-Action service-learning project, your school name, contact address, and telephone number. Be sure to include a brief overview of your project and copies of any other media coverage you have already received.

The use of the media is not just to promote your project, as a news agency. It can also be an effective tool in educating your community. For instance, you can each write articles informing the public about a certain aspect of your project. In researching monuments, one Community-Action team wrote informative articles about each of the dozen sculptures it researched. Included was a picture of the researcher/writer and the monument. This group also created several half-minute radio spots concerning each monument. Although this was not the ultimate goal of the project (restoring several of the monuments was), it raised the community's awareness and kept the group in the spotlight.

The Media Action Group should work closely with the Public Relations Action Group. Only by trying constantly to get your story in the media will your story reach the media. Remember to supply the *who, what, when, where,* and *how* in your press releases. Also remember that people really do want to hear good news. It is your group's responsibility to *pitch* it well. It's like fishing: the more you throw out the fishing line, the more fish you will hook!

CA

Documentation Action Group

Job Description

The Documentation Action Group plays a critical role in documenting the service-learning project from start to finish. From keeping the scrapbook and journal to taking and digitizing the photos and videos, scrapbooking, and filing everything, this group stays very busy. The members of this group should be organized and creative, with some able to use technology, such as digital cameras, video cameras, computers, and various software programs, effectively.

Within the Documentation Action Group are specific jobs: Digital Coordinator, Journalist, File Clerk, and Scrapbook Coordinator (see job descriptions). In addition to these jobs, this group may choose to select a photographer, videographer, and/or computer specialist, or those responsibilities can be shared among varying group members at different times. Working together, this group will produce a record of the service-learning experience. This is an important task, as grants, awards, and competitions for which the service-learning team may choose to apply all require accurate documentation of the team's actions and accomplishments.

Members of this group may require training in the different technologies it may choose to use, such as digital photography, videotaping, and how to use computers and software programs. Community partners who can help with this training could prove a valuable asset to this group. You may choose to divide this group into two subgroups: the technology group and the non-technology group. Included in the technology subgroup could be those involved in photography, videography, and computer technology. Included in the non-technology subgroup could be the File Clerk, the Scrapbook Coordinator, the Journalist, and the Chairperson.

Much is expected from this group all along the way, but no more than you can deliver!

CA

Digital Coordinator

Job Description

The Digital Coordinator's job is one of providing an accurate and thorough record of the action of the service-learning experience by digitalization. The person given this important task should be organized, creative, and independent. He or she should also be a member of the Documentation Action Group. The Documentation Action Group will assist you in many ways. As Digital Coordinator, you will decide which photos and videos should be made by the photographer and videographer (which can be alternated within the group, according to the determinations of the Digital Coordinator or the Documentation Action Group chairperson) and which ones should be digitized for final videos and slideshows. You are ultimately responsible for creating an accurate digital documentation of the project, bringing it alive as a real day-to-day operation as well as a completed project.

The digital pictures and videos taken should capture the creative and dynamic moments of the project—the many ideas from conception to conclusion. As Digital Coordinator, it is your responsibility to arrange the recording of groups working together; individuals doing different parts of the project; fellow students making phone calls, creating artwork, and even being silly from time to time.

It is important for you to make sure the *date* of each photograph or video is included. You must make sure the video is narrated during the recording or soon thereafter and must arrange for different people in all groups to be interviewed often about what they are doing during the course of the service-learning experience. Be sure to record any important events, such as field trips, guest speakers, and any presentations that may take place.

At the conclusion of the service-learning experience, you should have many photos as well as four to five full videos of the project, in addition to other types of digital representations. It is suggested that the Digital Coordinator coordinate the following tasks:

- Organization of the photographs or clips from the entire project, working with others within the group to compile it into one final video or slideshow presentation.

- Creation of *artsy* headings and titles for the various stages of the project that can be inserted into the video or slideshow in the appropriate places. You will work with the Media Action Group or the Public Relations Action Group on this task.

- Creation of a more polished final video, with dubbed-in narration where needed, as well as music. This task requires the proper equipment. If your school does not have the equipment needed, contact the video department of a local TV station or community college for technical support. They are often willing to offer their expertise and/or the equipment necessary for dubbing and finishing videos.

Be creative, have fun, and don't forget to smile!

CA

Press Secretary

Job Description

The Press Secretary's job is to read the *press releases* at the *press conferences*. The Press Secretary should be a member of the Media Action Group. This person should be able to *articulate* well. *Articulate* means to speak clearly. The press secretary should be neither shy nor easily distracted.

After reading the prepared statement, or Press Release, the Press Secretary will ask if the reporters have any questions. If the Press Secretary cannot answer a specific question asked by a reporter, he or she should know to whom the question should be directed and then ask that person to address the question (or ask, for example, "Would someone from the PR Group address that question?").

Tips:

- On the day of the press conference, dress up more than usual.
- Be familiar with the text of the press release, so that you can look out at the press corps. Make *eye contact* while you are delivering the press release.
- Watch the president's press secretary on TV at an official press conference.
- Be friendly. Smile, but don't be silly. Don't interrupt reporters while they are talking.
- Remember: *you* are in charge of the press conference. If any comments are to be made officially from the group (including your teacher), you should be the one *calling the shots* and directing the questions.

CA

File Clerk

Job Description

The File Clerk's job is an important one. A member of the Documentation Action Group, the File Clerk sets up and maintains the records for the entire service-learning project. All material concerning the project should be kept on file. The File Clerk continues to update the files throughout the project.

Two drawers of a filing cabinet will be necessary for the project. One will consist of a *drop file*, with separate folders for each element of the project. The other will consist of the scrapbook, videos, camera, and so on connected with the project.

Each project will require its own set of subjects to be filed. Among others, the following file folders will be needed:

- Correspondence
- Scrapbook information
- Press releases
- News articles
- Research
- Photographs and negatives
- Phone books
- Hall and phone passes
- Correspondence
- Press conference material (for example, banners)
- Project stationery
- Research information
- Miscellaneous

In addition to setting up and maintaining the files, you will also, toward the end of the project, compile a *Correspondence Notebook*. You will need a three-ring binder, the type with a plastic outer pocket. The Public Relations Action Group will design a cover insert to slide into this outer pocket. You will also need some clear plastic sheet protectors to hold each piece of correspondence. In chronological order, you will insert a copy of the letters you sent out and the letters you received. You can create a table of contents, but this is not essential.

CA

Journalist

Job Description

The Journalist's job is one of keeping a record of the action of the Community-Action Project. The person given this important task should be proficient at writing. At a minimum, entries should be recorded weekly. In addition to the weekly entry, the Journalist should make a record of any *special events*, such as *press conferences* or *speakers*.

It is important for the journalist to record the *date* at the top of the page. As with any journal or diary, the form should not be important. The most important aspect of this job is keeping a record of the progress of the group. Sentence structure or other grammar elements should not hinder this process, unless otherwise instructed by the teacher.

The Journalist should check with each group at the end of the week and record any progress made. For instance, "The Media Action Group sent out press releases to all local and area newspapers on Monday concerning the . . ."

The Journalist, a member of the Documentation Action Group, should be sure to make accurate entries concerning *guest speakers* or *visitors* to the class or *visits outside the classroom (i.e., field trips)*. Special care should be taken to correctly record the name of any guest, his or her title, and the information given by this guest.

The records kept by the Journalist will serve as a reference for the class when filling out grant or award applications; therefore, it is essential that the Journalist keep detailed records. The Journalist serves an important function in documenting through writing the entire service-learning experience.

CA

Scrapbook Coordinator

Job Description

The Scrapbook Coordinator's job, an important one in the Documentation Action Group, is to keep an accurate record of the action of the team by documenting the service-learning project. The person given this important task should be organized, creative, and independent.

The scrapbook should be a compilation of news articles, photographs, notes taken during the project, phone messages, scraps of ideas from groups—anything that will help document the project and bring it alive as a real day-to-day operation, not just a final project.

The scrapbook should capture the *creative* moments of the project—the ideas during conception. Brainstormed ideas jotted messily on torn paper, initial drawings in the project, research notes, and items such as these should be included in the Community-Action project scrapbook.

It is important for the Scrapbook Coordinator to record the *date* at the top of each page or section. Be sure to cut out the *name of the newspaper* and the *date of publication* with each article you clip.

The format will be left to you. You can organize it chronologically (according to time). You can also organize it according to subject. For instance, you can have one part consisting of research ideas; one part consisting of news articles about your group; and one part about day-to-day operations and notes.

Be creative in your presentation. Be precise as to what is in the scrapbook—label it well. Use color. Create collages of some of the events. Use photographs or drawings to illustrate the important happenings. Try to make your project come alive. If you like, you can get one or two others in the class to help.

CA

Job Selection Form
for Action Groups

Directions

Select the Action Group you would like to be a part of for your Community-Action service-learning experience. Rank your group preferences. Place a 1 in the blank beside the group you want to be in most. Place a 2 in the blank beside your second choice. Be sure to review the job descriptions before selecting your group preferences. Everyone will be assigned to a Research Group automatically in addition to an Action Group.

____ Media Action Group (includes job of Press Secretary)

____ Documentation Action Group (includes jobs of Digital Coordinator, Journalist, File Clerk, and Scrapbook Coordinator)

____ Public Relations Action Group

____ Correspondence Action Group

____ _____ Action Group (topic-specific action group—if needed)

____ _____ Action Group (topic-specific action group—if needed)

Note: each person will be assigned to one Action Group. Your preferences will be considered when assigning you to the Action Group. Facilitators (already selected) will not be assigned to any other group because their job is so demanding, and they must oversee all other groups.

CA

T-shirt Design

Directions

Create a design for the team T-shirt that will help to identify your class and project to the community. The design should be connected the goals of your project. Be sure to include your team name as part of the design. Use scrap paper to initially draft your design and then put your final design below.

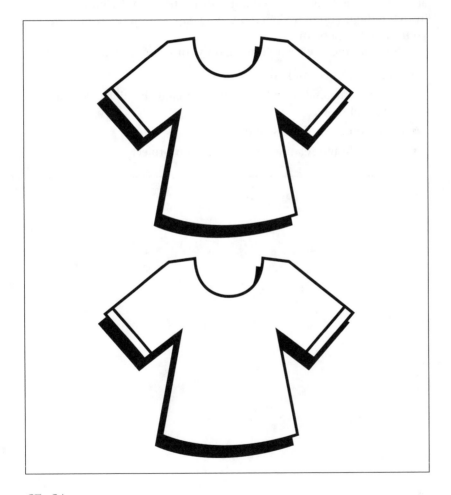

CE, CA

Designing Action Stationery

Directions

Design the stationery that will be used during your project. It should somehow connect to your project. You will design both the font and the artwork. If you'd like, both can be generated in an advanced graphics program on the computer. If your project is about *trash*, you might want to use some type of trash vehicle or a trash can. If it is about restoring buildings, you might want to use a design incorporating a building. You may sketch on scrap paper or on the computer. Put your final design below.

You *must* include the following on your stationery design:

- Name of project and group
- School name and complete address (include email or web address, if applicable)
- Phone number of the school
- Graphic design relating to you and your project

CE, CA

Telephone Tips

Proper phone etiquette is *essential* in order to get the cooperation you need as well as the credit you deserve for your service-learning project. Nothing leaves a worse impression than rudeness. These *tips* should help you during your phone contacts.

- Try to call your contacts during working hours, if possible. Absolutely *no* phone contacts should be made at night after 8:30 P.M. or in the morning before 9:00 A.M.!

- Always identify yourself individually at the beginning of the conversation and then as a member of your group or class.

- Be *specific* as to the nature of the phone call. State what it is you need from this phone contact.

- Be familiar with the topic before calling in case the person you have called asks questions. You don't want to appear uninformed.

- Use *magic phrases,* such as, "please," "thank you," and "we would appreciate it if you could . . ."

- In conclusion, thank the contact for his or her time and information, if you received information.

- Use *adult* manners, but still act like a *kid.* Adults can't resist helping *kids,* especially polite ones!

- If you need this person to get back in contact with you, do not forget to give him or her your teacher's return phone and/or fax number, email address, or your home phone number, if your parents permit it.

CS, CE, CA

Let's Talk

What Is an Interview?

An *interview* is a conversation in which facts or statements are obtained from someone. Interviews can be recorded either by taking notes or by tape or video recording.

Conducting interviews of knowledgeable persons can be an effective way to gather general research on your project area. Interviewing can also be an important method of confirming or acquiring additional project information.

Suggestions

- Set up the interview in advance by contacting the person in person or by telephone or email.
- Have your questions written or typed in advance. The questions should not be too lengthy.
- Be specific about the time and the place for the interview—and *don't be late!*
- Have everything set up in advance for the interview. If you are taping the interview, everything should be prepared and in place beforehand.
- Speak clearly and give the person time to respond.
- Remember to use *good manners* and *be pleasant.*
- You can, of course, deviate from the prepared questions; you may, in fact, need to do that as the interview proceeds, according to the responses.

CS, CE, CA

Meeting Tips

Don't Forget To:

- Call ahead—at least a week in advance—so that you can be put on the *agenda* of the meeting. As many of the group as possible should attend the meeting—the more the merrier and the more there, the more effective you will be.

- Select a spokesperson to represent the group and deliver the presentation prior to the meeting. The spokesperson should be *very* familiar with the presentation, be *dynamic*, and *smile.*

- Prepare a complete, concise, and creative presentation—but remember to *get to the point,* being as brief as you can, while still getting your message across.

- Let the spokesperson present the ideas your team has. If those in charge of the meeting ask for other ideas from the group, any of you who can add to the discussion should. It might be a good idea to *raise your hand* and be called on by the person or persons in charge of the meeting. Most meetings operate by certain rules of order—before the meeting, find out about those rules and follow them.

- Be early and sit together, but *not* next to your best friend. *No giggling!* Dress up a little more than usual. Sit still. *Don't squirm.* Act interested, *even if you're not.* Smile. Good impressions are very important—*and so are you!*

CS, CE, CA

Press Conference

Hot Tips

- Invite your principal and, perhaps, your superintendent and board of education members.
- Be sure your Digital Coordinator or a member of the Media or Documentation Action Group has arranged to take photographs and videos of the press conference for later publicity and documentation.
- Do not let the teacher take over—this is *your* press conference!
- Be sure to thank everyone for attending—remember your manners!
- Be on your very best behavior during the press conference.
- Create a press conference banner to use with all your press conferences. You should laminate it so it can be used again (see sample below).

CA

Role-playing the Action

The Challenge:
The Plan:

Brainstorm ideas for role-playing:

Before you begin role-playing, read the challenge and plan aloud to reconfirm your plan or request.

CE, CA

Our Skit Action Plan

The challenge the we would like to overcome is:

We recommend that . . . (briefly write out your plan in the space below):

Brainstorm ideas for the skit that you will do to present your recommended action plan. The skit should be brief and, above all, fun!

Before performing your skit, first read the challenge and action plan aloud (in box at top of page).

CE, CA

Tracking the Service Experience

Student Name: _____ Total Hours: _____

Project Name: _____

Type of Service-Learning Activity

❏ Individual   ❏ Group

❏ Volunteer activity   ❏ Volunteer activity

❏ Individual project   ❏ Group project

❏ Internship

Level of Service-Learning

❏ Community-Service

❏ Community-Exploration

❏ Community-Action

Service Hours

Week of	In-school	On-site	Meetings

CS, CE, CA

Action Self-Evaluation

Name: _____

Criteria for Evaluation

Circle the number in each area that best reflects the amount of work you have done on this project for this period. Your grade will be the total of the numbers circled in the five areas multiplied by two.

(Scale 1–10)

| | Lousy | Super |

Lousy ◄———————————————————► Super

1. Initiative
(Go-getter)

1 2 3 4 5 6 7 8 9 10

2. Organization
(Planning, goals)

1 2 3 4 5 6 7 8 9 10

3. Follow-through
(Accomplishments)

1 2 3 4 5 6 7 8 9 10

4. Time on task
(Gets to work early and works until the end)

1 2 3 4 5 6 7 8 9 10

5. Commitment
(Interest in project)

1 2 3 4 5 6 7 8 9 10

Grade: [   ]   Total: [   ]

CS, CE, CA

Weekly Action Report

Name(s): _____

Directions

In the space below, note the service-learning activities that you have been involved in this week. *Be specific.*

_____

_____

_____

_____

_____

In the space below, list the accomplishments for this week *briefly.*

1 _____

2 _____

3 _____

4 _____

Signature(s): _____

_____

_____

Date: _____   Grade for this week: _____

Note: teacher comments written on back!

CS, CE, CA

Service-Learning Reflection Rubric: Observation

Student Name: _____

Level 1 Criteria: *Observation*	Beginning 1	Developing 2	Accomplished 3	Exemplary 4	Score
Shares general observations about experience (quality is not a factor)					
Gives concrete examples (minimum of two) of observed behaviors or characteristics of the individuals or the setting (insight is not required)					
Relates personal beliefs about situation (at least two)					
Recognizes different points of view					
				Total Score	

Beginning—description of identifiable performance characteristics reflecting a beginning level of performance
Developing—description of identifiable performance characteristics reflecting development and movement toward mastery of performance
Accomplished—description of identifiable performance characteristics reflecting mastery of performance
Exemplary—description of identifiable performance characteristics reflecting the highest level of performance

CS

156

Service-Learning Reflection Rubric: Analysis

Student Name: _____

Level 2 Criteria: *Analysis*	Beginning 1	Developing 2	Accomplished 3	Exemplary 4	Score
Reflections are fairly comprehensive with some aware-ness of the subtle shades of meaning without necessarily considering the broader situation					
Provides a convincing perspective although not necessarily connecting beyond the immediate experience or to factors that illustrate how difficult change is to accomplish					
Provides *personal belief* as well as *evidence* and shows a be-ginning ability to explain the difference between the two					
Shows an understanding of justifiable differences of perspective					
Displays an emerging capacity to understand and inter-pret evidence					
				Total Score	

Beginning—description of identifiable performance characteristics reflecting a beginning level of performance

Developing—description of identifiable performance characteristics reflecting development and movement toward mastery of performance

Accomplished—description of identifiable performance characteristics reflecting mastery of performance

Exemplary—description of identifiable performance characteristics reflecting the highest level of performance

CE

Service-Learning Reflection Rubric: Synthesis

Student Name: _____

Level 3 Criteria: *Synthesis*	Beginning 1	Developing 2	Accomplished 3	Exemplary 4	Score
Looks at things from a variety of viewpoints and able to put into context perceived differences within the situation					
Is capable of appreciating conflicting ideas within the situation and of understanding that these ideas can be assessed					
Understands that actions vary by situation and is able to recognize the many issues that affect his or her decision making					
Formulates conclusions based on critical thinking and evidence					
Evaluates the importance of the decisions facing the individuals and/or community involved and of his or her responsibility as a part of it all					
				Total Score	

Beginning—description of identifiable performance characteristics reflecting a beginning level of performance

Developing—description of identifiable performance characteristics reflecting development and movement toward mastery of performance

Accomplished—description of identifiable performance characteristics reflecting mastery of performance

Exemplary—description of identifiable performance characteristics reflecting the highest level of performance

CA

May be copied for classroom use. © 2007 by Alice W. Terry and Jann E. Bohnenberger, from Service-Learning . . . by Degrees (Heinemann: Portsmouth, NH).

158

Preliminary Reflection Rubric for Community-Service

Student Name: _____

Preliminary Community-Service Reflection Rubric	🙁 Beginning 1	🙂 Developing 2	😊 Accomplished 3	😄 Excellent 4	Points
Describes what happened during the experience					
Describes the people who were involved in the experience					
Shares one part of the experience that was meaningful					
Shares feelings about the experience					
				Total Points	

Comments: _____

_____

_____

CS

159

Appendix B

Developmental Service-Learning Typology

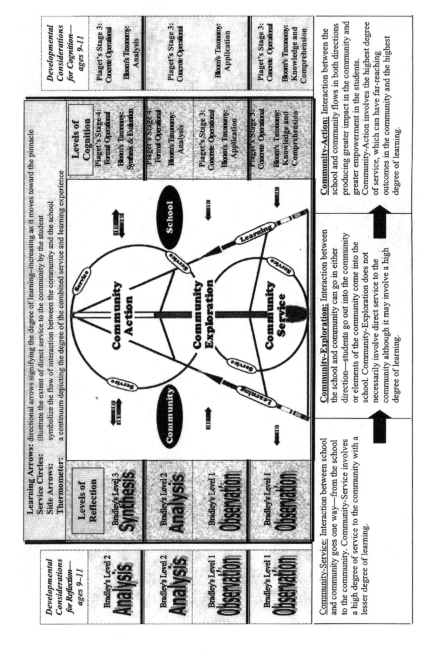

Table of Types of Service-Learning

Type of Service-Learning	Activities	Best-Practice Model for Teachers	Reflective Questions	Effects
Community-Action Highest degree of service and learning	• Civic Reform: legislative initiatives, school reform, health and human services • Professional Services: historic nominations, grant-writing models for community improvement • Community Enhancement: renewal and restoration, cultural and aesthetic ventures, environmental improvements	• At this level, Preparation, Action, Reflection, and Celebration are interwoven throughout the project instead of implemented as separate steps • Creative problem solving • Cognitive apprenticeship model • Cooperative learning strategies • Synthesis-level reflection • Celebration	Synthesis-level examples: • What could be combined or modified to improve the outcome? • What methods would you use to assess the importance, success, and value of your ideas and actions? • How would you defend your decisions to others, including your community partners and the service recipients?	• Empowerment • Individual and societal awareness, impact, and understanding • Creative thinking • Community improvement • Perseverance • Effects include those listed on lower levels • Synthesis and evaluation

(continued)

163

Type of Service-Learning	Activities	Best-Practice Model for Teachers	Reflective Questions	Effects
Community-Exploration Varying degree of service and learning	• Internships, cooperative programs, field experiences • Community information-gathering/ interpretation	• Preparation: Facilitate topical discussion, brainstorming ideas • Action (exploration of community): Monitor research; application/ analysis of research; product • Analysis-level reflection • Celebration	Analysis-level examples: (see Community-Service for Observation examples) • How would you organize the information acquired to show your understanding of the community need? • What is the relationship between this situation and others that are similar or quite different?	• Individual and societal awareness and understanding • Career development, self-esteem, risk taking, self-motivation • Effects vary according to activity • Vary degrees of direct and/or indirect service • Application and analysis
Community-Service High degree of service, lower level of learning	• Tutoring • Picking up trash on highways • Serving food at a homeless shelter or mission • Working with senior citizens • Shelving books at a library • Other similar types of volunteer activities	• Preparation: Facilitate brainstorming of service ideas, contact service recipients • Action (direct service to community): Monitor service experience • Observation-level reflection • Celebration	Observation-level examples: • What have you observed about this community situation? • Who were the main participants? List the service provider, service recipient, and community partner.	• Risk taking, moral development, self-confidence, positive self-esteem, personal and social growth, altruism, civic participation, self-efficacy, improvement of school attendance • Individual awareness • Knowledge and comprehension

*The level of reflection impacts the effects demonstrated.

Note: it is feasible that two students working on the same activity could function at conjoining levels of reflection.

Service-Learning Resources

The following list contains readily available materials that may help you in facilitating your service-learning project. These listings can be accessed through the Internet and are designed to provide tools, materials, and resources to aid teachers in implementing service-learning in their classroom.

CNCS EpiCenter: sponsored by the Corporation for National and Community Service. This site supports the development of sustainable programs by sharing what works in community service and volunteering. Offers examples of effective practices in service-learning. Website: http://nationalservice.org/resources/epicenter/

Compact for Learning and Citizenship: a nationwide coalition of chief state school officers, district superintendents, and educators committed to service-learning in K–12 classrooms. Download service-learning articles and tool kits on this Compact for Learning and Citizenship page: www.ecs.org/html/projectsPartners/clc/CLCPublications.asp

Constitutional Rights Foundation—Service-learning Network: explores the fundraising process in relation to service-learning, how to write grants. Contains many service-learning resources. Website: www.crf-usa.org/network/net7_4.html

Corporation for National and Community Service—Learn and Serve America: information on the service-learning resources, training, and grants available to schools through the Learn and Serve America program. Website: www.learnandserve.org.

Idealist.org—Action Without Borders: sponsors a site that introduces youth to worldwide nonprofit agencies and encourages young people to get involved in their community through supporting an established agency. Great resources for teachers and students from getting organized to funding your project. Website: www.idealist.org/. Website for youth to volunteer: www.idealist.org/kat/volunteercenter.html

Learning In Deed: a project of the WK Kellogg Foundation, longtime advocate of service-learning. This page offers a listing of websites with service-learning lesson plans: www.learningindeed.org/tools/other/currnet.html

National Service-Learning Clearinghouse: many resources for K–12 service-learning including a listing of funding sources, latest research, books, references, and agencies. Website: www.servicelearning.org

National Service-Learning Partnership: a national network of members advancing service-learning as a core part of education. The site offers many tools, resources, and best practices for teachers and community members. Website: www.service-learningpartnership.org

National Youth Leadership Council: find out about model programs, curricula, and youth training for schools across America at this website. Teachers may order fee-based products such as the Essential Elements of Service-Learning. Website: http://nylc.org/

Northwest Regional Education Laboratory: offers service-learning information, practices, and a toolbox that provides guidelines to begin and maintain your service-learning program, includes work pages and checklists. Essential Elements of Service Learning: www.nwrel.org/ruraled /learnserve/resources/essential_1.pdf. Toolbox: www.nwrel.org /ruraled/learnserve/resources/SL_Toolbox.pdf

Points of Light Foundation: promotes community service and volunteering in the United States through a program called *Everyone Wins When Youth Serve*. Website: www.pointsoflight.org

SEANet: a national network of staff from state education agencies and organizations that provide leadership on K–12 service-learning. Site offers numerous service-learning resources including the latest information from the state education agencies. Website: http://seanetonline.org

TeachNet: a great resource when designing a service-learning lesson plan for your students. This site offers sample service-learning lesson plans in many different content areas, ideas for reflection and celebration, and information on available service-learning grants. Website: www.teachnet.com

Youth Service America: promotes youth volunteering by supporting organizations that are dedicated to youth service issues. Find out about YSA initiatives such as National Youth Service Day, the President's Student Service Challenge, and the Fund for Social Entrepreneurs. Be sure to check out "Project Plan-It," an interactive online tool to create service-learning projects. Website: www.ysa.org/

Opportunities for Celebration and Demonstration

Great ideas for helping youth celebrate the positive difference they have made in their community!

Many local and national businesses, clubs, organizations, and government agencies recognize the efforts made by students to improve their community and the world around them. The awards range from certificates of recognition to cash prizes for individual or group efforts. To find out specifics about each competition, please contact the organization directly at the following addresses. In addition, you may want to check with local youth groups, fraternal or civic organizations, churches, educational resource centers, or the community affairs department of local colleges or universities to find out about opportunities for recognition available locally.

American Health Care Association—Public Relations Office, 1201 L St., NW, Washington, DC 20005. "Young Adult Volunteer of the Year" honors volunteer work done in nursing homes. Must be nominated by state health care association.

Bayer/National Science Foundation Award—www.nsf.gov/bayer-nsf-award.html. Youth organizations and sixth, seventh, and eighth graders are eligible. Four students work together to solve a community problem. Awards include a $25,000 community grant, a trip to Disney World, and savings bonds for student team members.

Boys and Girls Clubs of America—www.bgca.org/members/youth_of_year.asp. "National Youth of the Year Award" to members for contributions to home, school, church, community, and boys and girls clubs. Local, state, regional, and national winner. Scholarships sponsored by *Reader's Digest*.

Colgate Youth for America Award—www.colgate.com. P.O. Box 1058, FDR Station, New York, NY 10150-1058. Students must be involved in Boy Scouts/Girls Scouts, Boys Club/Girls Club, 4-H Clubs, or Campfire. March 15 deadline. A total of 315 cash awards.

Congressional Award—www.congressionalaward.org. Award program of the U.S. Congress for students aged fourteen to twenty-three. Certificates and medals for volunteer public service.

Daily Point of Light Award—www.pointsoflight.org/dpol/ProgramInfo.html. Awards given daily to those who have made a service commitment to meet critical community needs.

Future Problem Solving Program—www.fpsp.org. P.O. Box 2470, Melbourne, FL 32902. Students must be registered in the Community Problem Solving Program through their local affiliate. Awards and trophies at the Affiliate and International level of competition for outstanding group and individual community projects. Annual International Conference celebrating the best community projects.

The Giraffe Project—www.giraffe.org. P.O. Box 759, Langley, WA 98260. Recognizes individuals and groups who "stick their neck out" for the betterment of society.

Keep America Beautiful, Inc.—www.kab.org. Contact the Awards Program Coordinator, 1010 Washington Blvd., 7th Fl., Stamford, CT 06901. Individual and group awards for projects on environmental improvements. August deadline.

National Service-Learning Leader Schools—www.leaderschools.org. Recognizes junior and senior high schools for excellence in service-learning.

Points of Light Foundation—www.pointsoflight.org/forvolunteer/awards.cfm. Site offers a lengthy listing of individual and group awards for youth involved in community service.

Presidential Freedom Scholarships—www.nationalservice/scholarships.org. Each high school in the United States may select two students (juniors or seniors) to receive a $1,000 scholarship for outstanding leadership in service to the community.

President's Student Service Award—www.students-service-awards.org /awards-index.htm. Honors full-time students from kindergarten through college who contribute at least 100 hours (50 hours for younger students) of service to the community.

Prudential Spirit of the Community Awards—www.prudential.com /community. Awarded by Prudential Financial Services. Recognizes middle- and high-school students who have demonstrated exemplary, self-initiated community service.

REACT Take Action Award—www.react.com. Five student scholarships for significant contribution to their schools, communities, and nation.

SeaWorld/Busch Gardens Environmental Excellence Awards—www.seaworld .org. SeaWorld Adventure Park, Education Department, 7007 SeaWorld Dr., Orlando, FL 32821. K–12 students can submit environmental projects and win cash awards. January deadline.

Seventeen Magazine/Cover Girl Volunteerism Awards—E-mail: cyberscoop@ seventeen.com. P.O. Box 9383, Des Moines, IA 50306. Recognizes and awards scholarships to youth who have made significant contributions to their community.

Target Stores All-Around Scholarship—Contact the Target All-Around Scholarship program manager, 1-800-537-4180. Over 1,000 scholarships for community service. Essay required.

YouthActionNet—http://www.youthactionnet.org/minigrants.php. Awards minigrants of $500 for projects that bring about positive social change and youth leadership.

References

Alliance for Service Learning in Education Reform. 1993. *Standards of Quality and Excellence for School-Based Service Learning*. Washington, DC: Council of Chief State School Officers.

Bloom, Benjamin S., ed. 1956. *Taxonomy of Educational Objectives: The Classification of Educational Goals: Handbook I, Cognitive Domain*. New York: Longmans, Green.

Bohnenberger, Jann, and Alice W. Terry. 2002. "Community Problem Solving Works for Middle Level Students." *Middle School Journal* 34 (1): 5–12.

Boyer, Ernest L. 1995. *The Basic School: A Community for Learning*. Princeton, NJ: Carnegie Endowment for the Advancement of Teaching.

Bradley, James. 1995. "A Model for Evaluating Student Learning in Academically Based Service." In *Connecting Cognition and Action: Evaluation of Student Performance in Service Learning Courses*, edited by M. Troppe, 13–26. Providence, RI: Campus Compact.

Brown, John Seely, Allan Collins, and Paul Duguid. 1989. "Situated Cognition and the Culture of Learning." *Educational Researcher* 18 (1): 32–42.

Cairn, Rich. 2003. *Partner Power and Service Learning: Manual for Community-Based Organizations to Work with Schools* ServeMinnesota! [cited March 15, 2006.]

Carnegie Council on Adolescent Development. 1989. *Turning Points: Preparing American Youth for the 21st Century*. New York: Carnegie Corporation of New York.

Close Up Foundation, 1995 [cited May 15, 2006]. Available from http://servicelearning.org/lib_svcs/bibs/cb_bibs/sl_glance/index.php?search_term="Standards%20of%20quality%20for%20school-based%20and%20community-based%20service-learning.

Conrad, Dan, and Diane Hedin. 1991. "Service: A Pathway to Knowledge." *Journal of Cooperative Education* 27 (2): 73–84.

Dewey, John. 1954. *The Public and Its Problems*. Athens, OH: Swallow Press.

Fiske, Edward B. 2002. "Learning in Deed: The Power of Service-Learning for American Schools." National Commission on Service-Learning.

"Franklin Co. 'Green Gang' Kids Talk Trash and Save Their County Money." *Athens Daily News*, March 8 1993, 3.

Fredericks, Linda. 2002. "Learning that Lasts: How Service-Learning Can Become an Integral Part of Schools, States, and Communities." Education Commission of the States [cited September 20 2006]. Available from www.ecs.org/html/ProjectsPartners/nclc/NCLC_Publications.asp

Gates, Bill. 2005. "Keynote Address." In *National Summit on High Schools.* Washington DC.

Henderson, Bruce. 1987. "The Kids Who Saved a Dying Town." *Reader's Digest,* September: 42–46.

Johnson, Rheta Grimsley. 1995. "Hard Rock Kids Are as Good as Granite." *The Atlanta Journal and The Atlanta Constitution,* January 8, 1995, B1.

Joiner, K. 1999. "Walking Through History. . . ." *Serving to Learn* 1 (2): 1–9.

Kinsley, Carol W., and Kate McPherson. 1995. *Enriching the Curriculum Through Service Learning.* Alexandria, VA: Association for Supervision and Curriculum Development.

Kluth, Paula. 2000. "Community-Referenced Learning and the Inclusive Classroom." *Remedial & Special Education* 21 (1): 19–27.

Lickona, Thomas. 1996. "Eleven Principles of Effective Character Education." *Journal of Moral Education* 25 (1): 93–100.

McCarthy, Rebecca. 1993. "Kids Talk Trash, and It Saves the County Money." *The Atlanta Journal/The Atlanta Constitution,* March 7 1993, D1.

National and Community Service Act of 1990. 1991. Pub. L. No. 101-610, 42 USC 12401; 104 Stat. 3127.

National Council for the Social Studies. *About NCSS* [cited September 10 2006]. Available from http://www.ncss.org/about/.

National Middle School Association. 2003. *This We Believe: Successful Schools for Young Adolescents.* Westerville, OH: National Middle School Association.

Muth, K. Denise, and Donna E. Alvermann. 1998. *Teaching and Learning in the Middle Grades.* 2nd ed. Boston, MA: Allyn & Bacon.

Nickerson, R. S., ed. 1994. *The Teaching of Thinking and Problem Solving.* Edited by R.J. Sternberg, *Thinking and Problem Solving.* San Diego, CA: Academic Press.

Osborn, Alex. 1963. *Creative Imagination.* 3rd ed. New York: Charles Scribner.

Parnes, Sidney. 1967. *Creative Behavior Guidebook.* New York: Charles Scribner.

Passow, A. Harry. 1989. "Educating Gifted Persons Who Are Caring and Concerned." *Gifted Education International* 6 (1): 5–7.

Pearson, Sarah. 2002. *Finding Common Ground: Service-Learning and Education Reform: A Survey of 28 Leading School Reform Models.* Washington, DC: American Youth Policy Forum.

Piaget, Jean. 1950. *The Psychology of Intelligence.* San Diego: Harcourt Brace Jovanovich.

Schine, Joan. 1996. "Service Learning: A Promising Strategy for Connecting Students to Communities." *Middle School Journal* 28 (2): 3–9.

———, ed. 1997. *Service Learning*. Chicago: The University of Chicago.

Slavin, Robert E. 1986. "Cooperative Learning: Engineering Social Psychology in the Classroom." In *The Social Psychology of Education: Current Research and Theory*, edited by R. S. Feldman. Cambridge, England: Cambridge University.

Standards of Quality for School-Based Service-Learning. 1995. In, ed. Alliance for Service-Learning in Educational Reform. Close Up Foundation, http://servicelearning.org/lib_svcs/bibs/sl_glance/index.php?search_term="Standards%20for%school-based%20and%20community-based%20service-learning (accessed May 19, 2006).

"Students Have Ideas for Landfill." *The NEWS Leader*, March 7, 1991, 13.

Terry, Alice Wickersham. 2000. "A Case Study of Community Action Service Learning on Young, Gifted Adolescents and Their Community." (Doctoral dissertation, University of Georgia). *Dissertation Abstracts International, 61,* (08), 3058.

Terry, Alice W. 2000. "An Early Glimpse: Service Learning from an Adolescent Perspective." *The Journal of Secondary Gifted Education* 11 (3): 155–34.

Terry, Alice W., and Jann Bohnenberger. 1995. *The Complete How-to Book for Community Action Projects*. Knoxville, TN: ABLE Press.

Tomlinson, Carol Ann. 1999. *Differentiated Classroom: Responding to the Needs of All Learners*. Alexandria, VA: Association for Supervision and Curriculum Development.

Toole, Pamela, ed. 1998. *Essential Elements of Service-Learning*. St. Paul, Minnesota: National Youth Leadership Council.

Torrance, E. Paul. 1995. *Why Fly?* Norwood, NJ: Ablex Publishing Corporation.

"Way to go!" 1994. *Teen* (September): 128–31.

Webb, Norman. 1999. "Alignment of Science and Mathematics Standards and Assessments in Four States: Research Monograph No. 18."

Wheeler, Adrienne. 1994. "The Donahue Show." New York: National Broadcasting Company, July 22, 1994.

Yoder, Denise, Esther Retish, and Rahima Wade. 1996. "Service Learning: Meeting Student and Community Needs." *Teaching Exceptional Children* 28: 14–18.